500 Raku

500 Raku

Bold Explorations of a Dynamic Ceramics Technique

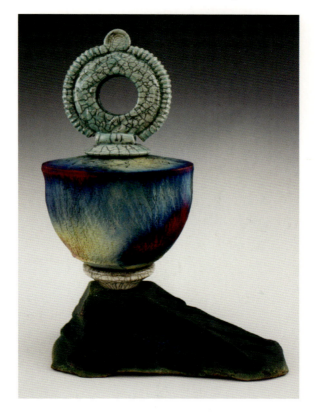

LARK CRAFTS

An Imprint of Sterling Publishing Co., Inc.
New York

WWW.LARKCRAFTS.COM

SENIOR EDITOR
Ray Hemachandra

EDITOR
Julie Hale

ART DIRECTOR
Matt Shay

JUROR
Jim Romberg

COVER DESIGNER
Kristi Pfeffer

TITLE PAGE
Gina Mars
Ritual Vessel, 2009

OPPOSITE
Fred Yokel
How'd This Happen?, 2007

FRONT COVER
Shelby Banks Duensing
Boxed In, 2005

BACK COVER, CLOCKWISE FROM TOP
Dave Deal
Boni Deal
Heron/Moon Wall Platter, 2008

Ann Testa
Pears on a Tray, 2008

Billy Ray Mangham
Berger Engblon—Petty Theft, 2009

SPINE
Charles Haile
Mythology of Dreams, 2006

FRONT FLAP
Dan Dudley
Mariachi, 2008

BACK FLAP
Michael Lancaster
Disc One Disc Two, 2009

Library of Congress Cataloging-in-Publication Data

500 raku : bold explorations of a dynamic ceramics technique. / author, Ray Hemachandra
     p. cm.
   Includes index.
   ISBN 978-1-60059-294-2 (pb-pbk. with flaps : alk. paper)
   1. Raku pottery. 2. Pottery--21st century. I. Title: Five hundred raku.
   NK4340.R3A15 2011
   738.3'7--dc22
                                              2010019178

10 9 8 7 6 5 4 3

Published by Lark Crafts
An Imprint of Sterling Publishing Co., Inc.
387 Park Avenue South, New York, NY 10016

Text © 2011, Lark Crafts, an Imprint of Sterling Publishing Co., Inc.
Photography © 2011, Artist/Photographer

Distributed in Canada by Sterling Publishing,
c/o Canadian Manda Group, 165 Dufferin Street
Toronto, Ontario, Canada M6K 3H6

Distributed in the United Kingdom by GMC Distribution Services,
Castle Place, 166 High Street, Lewes, East Sussex, England BN7 1XU

Distributed in Australia by Capricorn Link (Australia) Pty Ltd.,
P.O. Box 704, Windsor, NSW 2756 Australia

The works represented in this book are the original creations of the contributing artists. All artists retain copyright on their individual works.

The photographs and text in this volume are intended for the personal use of the reader and may be reproduced for that purpose only. Any other use, especially commercial use, is forbidden under law without written permission of the copyright holder.

If you have questions or comments about this book, please contact:
Lark Crafts
67 Broadway
Asheville, NC 28801
828-253-0467

Manufactured in China

All rights reserved

ISBN 13: 978-1-60059-294-2

For information about custom editions, special sales, and premium and corporate purchases, please contact the Sterling Special Sales Department at 800-805-5489 or specialsales@sterlingpub.com.

For information about desk and examination copies available to college and university professors, requests must be submitted to academic@larkbooks.com. Our complete policy can be found at www.larkcrafts.com.

Contents

Introduction by Jim Romberg   **6**

The Raku   **8**

About the Juror   **416**

Acknowledgments   **416**

Contributing Artists   **417**

Introduction

Since its development in Japan in the late sixteenth century, raku has united the spirituality of aesthetic contemplation with the science of ceramics. Thanks to the unique firing and post-firing procedures that characterize the technique, raku forms feature unique, one-of-a-kind effects that reflect not only the vision of the ceramist but also the engagement of a natural process—one that makes heat, fire, and smoke part of the artist's final statement.

Raku is a discipline that lends itself to invention and experimentation. As the pieces collected here prove, it remains a vibrant, lively medium after five centuries. Whether controlled and refined or speculative and unresolved, raku ware reflects a range of creative approaches and viewpoints. Contemporary artists use the technique to create a variety of forms, including vessels, sculpture, multimedia pieces, and installations, and they make the most of inventive surface treatments.

Janine Parent
Double Wall | 2008

Constantly evolving in content as well as process, raku has long been viewed as both a philosophical and an aesthetic approach to ceramics, and this duality gives it special appeal. In sixteenth-century Japan, raku epitomized the concept of *wabi*, the rustic simplicity of natural execution that ceramists articulated through the functional tea bowl. Embedded in Japanese culture since that time, raku has long been closely involved with the tea ceremony, an influential social and cultural institution. Raku expression in ceramics now has such aesthetic esteem that vessels from the sixteenth century are considered priceless treasures. The special creative spirit embodied by raku ware—a balance of simplicity and sophistication that goes beyond function—continues to enliven contemporary work in the medium.

Raku arrived in the United States in the 1950s as part of the "clay revolution," when the excitement of social and artistic change characterized by jazz and abstract expressionism found its way to ceramics. Clay was used in new ways during this time as an expressive medium. Quickly spreading through the studio and university ceramic communities, raku ignited a new spirit of invention among Western artists, who referred to raku's Eastern origins in their work and also used it to explore new forms and surfaces.

Alistair Danhieux
Grande Disque | 2009

Nina Kellogg
Red, Yellow, Orange in Black and White | 2005

In the 1950s, the vocabulary of the medium was expanded to include naked raku, a technique that remains popular today. Naked raku makes use of a clay slip, which peels away during the firing process. When the fired piece has cooled, the ceramist can scrape off or scratch through the slip that remains to create different textures and designs. With its refinement and subtle integration of form and surface, naked raku makes possible the construction of remarkably delicate figures and vessels. Janine Parent's *Double Wall* and Alistair Danhieux's *Grande Disque* are two of many pieces that feature the precise detailing and wonderful color contrast that result from naked raku.

The essence of raku is being expressed today in new and modern ways, from the figurative to the conceptual. In this book you'll see vessels that have wonderful presence paired with figures that inspire contemplation. You'll see large installations that employ raku on a grand scale, and intimate pieces that are driven by humor and social issues. Strong, emphatic works like Nina Kellogg's *Red, Yellow, Orange in Black and White* and Ana England's *Shared Identity: Wave and Galaxy with Thumbprints* use raku to make bold statements. Alessandro Gallo's *Rocky Raku* (page 8) and Stephen M. Braun's *Talking Trash* (page 410) are smart, satirical pieces that celebrate absurdity. What unites all of the works is a strong sense of the past and a devotion to craft.

In selecting pieces for the book, I considered more than 2,100 submissions. I gravitated toward work that seemed to preserve the customs of raku while pushing it to new frontiers. The selected artists have dramatically expanded the technique's aesthetic vocabulary while demonstrating astounding skill with surface, form, and firing. Their reverence for tradition combined with their thirst for experimentation ensures that raku will continue to flourish for years to come. I'm proud to share their work with you.

— Jim Romberg, juror

Ana England
Shared Identity: Wave and Galaxy with Thumbprints | 2006

Alessandro Gallo
Rocky Raku | 2009
19 x 28 x 24 INCHES (48.3 x 71.1 x 61 CM)
Hand-built ABF Sculpture High-Fire Clay,
brushed glaze, gas fired, smoking for reduction
PHOTO BY ARTIST

Julie Woodrow
Double-Walled Bowl | 2009
6 X 10 X 9½ INCHES (15.2 X 25.4 X 24.1 CM)
Thrown and altered white stoneware, dipped and poured glaze, carved, gas fired, smoking for reduction
PHOTO BY MARK STEELE

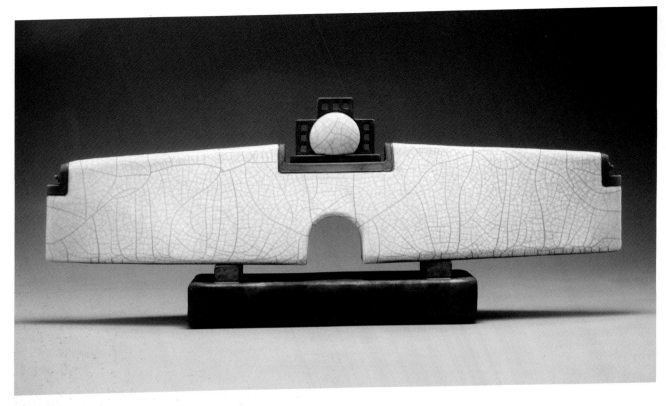

Steve Vachon
Horizon Vessel | 2009
8½ X 22¾ X 4 INCHES (21.6 X 57.8 X 10.2 CM)
Press-molded, hand-built, and slab-built personal-recipe clay, sprayed glaze, gas fired, smoking for reduction
PHOTO BY ARTIST

Leslie Green
Streambed | 2009
11 X 12 X 1 INCHES (27.9 X 30.5 X 2.5 CM)
Slab-built personal-recipe clay, brushed glaze, tossed slab texture,
gas-fired raku, controlled cooling, smoking for reduction
PHOTO BY GARY G. GIBSON

Bia Camargo
Maricotas | 2009
16 X 10 X 5 INCHES (40.6 X 25.4 X 12.7 CM)
Slab-built and hand-built white stoneware, dipped, brushed, stamped, gas fired, smoking for reduction
PHOTO BY FLAVIO LICO

Burcu Öztürk Karabey
Secret Boxes | 2009
11 13/16 X 39 5/8 INCHES (30 X 100 CM)
Slip-cast commercial clay, poured
glaze, gas fired, smoking for reduction
PHOTO BY SERDAR PEHLIVAN

Drew Gaede
Untitled | 2009
5½ X 6½ X 4½ INCHES (14 X 16.5 X 11.4 CM)
Slab-built Biz Bod, brushed glaze, stamped, gas fired, smoking for reduction
PHOTO BY PAUL F. MORRIS

Michael Prokos
Untitled | 2008
16¼ X 16¾ X 5½ INCHES (41.3 X 42.5 X 14 CM)
Slab-built personal-recipe clay, poured glaze,
gas fired, smoking for reduction, cone 06
PHOTO BY MARGO GEIST

Mike Yarnold
Untitled | 2009
8 X 7 X 7 INCHES (20.3 X 17.8 X 17.8 CM)
Wheel thrown, dipped glaze, wax-resist brushwork, gas fired, smoking for reduction
PHOTO BY ARTIST

Aki Onodera
El Sueño | 2009
EACH: 13 X 13 X 2 INCHES (33 X 33 X 5.1 CM)
Hand-built clay, brushed glaze interior, hand-built kiln firing with charcoal, no-reduction air cooling
PHOTO BY RAUL GALUSCA

Wilson H. Apkariah
Ramses | 2008
21 X 9 X 4½ INCHES (53.3 X 22.9 X 11.4 CM)
Hand-built raku, brushed glaze, sculpted,
gas fired, smoking for reduction
PHOTO BY WESLEY HARVEY

Julia Nicole Feld
Abstract in Red and Black | 2007
9 X 6½ X 7 INCHES (22.9 X 16.5 X 17.8 CM)
Hand-built Laguna Sculpture Raku, brushed and sponged glaze, carved, gas fired, smoking for reduction, cone 06
PHOTO BY ARTIST

Lisa Joanne Skog
Turquoise Bowl | 2009
11 X 3 INCHES (27.9 X 7.6 CM)
Wheel-thrown Sheba Raku, brushed, sprayed, and splashed glazes, gas fired, heavy smoking and reduction
PHOTO BY SHEILA CLENNELL

Rosemarie Greedy
Untitled | 2008
3½ X 3½ X 11 INCHES (8.9 X 8.9 X 27.9 CM)
Thrown and altered Laguna WSO, brushed glaze,
carbonized emu feather and horsehair, gas fired,
quick smoking, ferric chloride post-firing spray

PHOTO BY YURI AKUNEY

Margot McCartney
Nefertiti | 2007
40 x 18 INCHES (101.6 x 45.7 CM)
Hand-built paper clay, brushed glaze,
gas fired, no-reduction air cooling
PHOTO BY TED MILLER

Nancy Pené
New Horizons | 2006
5½ X 7 X 7 INCHES (14 X 17.8 X 17.8 CM)
Wheel-thrown Laguna WC-397 and WS-5, brushed glaze,
propane fired, post-reduction of paper and hardwood sawdust
PHOTO BY DAVID HANKINS

Martha Rieger
My Melting Pot | 2006
LARGEST: 20 X 10 INCHES (50.8 X 25.4 CM)
Wheel-thrown K129 Raku, burnished, slurry slip, raku glaze, terra sigillata, handmade stickers, gas fired, naked raku
PHOTO BY ERETZ ISRAEL MUSEUM

Philippe A. Buraud
Untitled | 2007

10½ X 12½ X 2½ INCHES (26.7 X 31.8 X 6.4 CM)

Slab-built and wheel-thrown Ceradel GT 100 X, brushed and sprayed glaze, gas fired, smoking for reduction

PHOTO BY ARTIST

Emily Jo Lees
Untitled | 2007

7 X 6¼ X 2½ INCHES (17.8 X 15.9 X 6.4 CM)

Slab-built, slump molded, assembled, and pinched Highwater Raku, brushed glaze, underglaze brushwork, gas-fired raku, smoking for reduction, 1850°F (1010°C)

PHOTO BY SETH TICE-LEWIS

Penny Truitt
Finding Balance | 2007
12 X 4½ X 25 INCHES (30.5 X 11.4 X 63.5 CM)
Slab-built personal-recipe clay, sprayed glaze, oxide wash, gas fired, selective smoking for reduction
PHOTO BY ADDISON DOTY

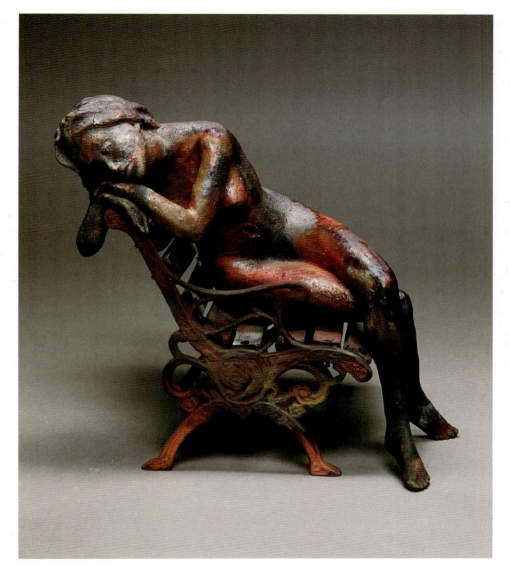

Helaine Schneider
Lost in a Daydream | 2005
9 x 11 x 8 INCHES (22.9 x 27.9 x 20.3 CM)
Hand-built and slab-built Max's Raku, brushed glaze,
electric fired, gas fired, smoking for reduction, cone 06
PHOTO BY ARTIST

Steven Branfman
Jared's Teabowl, 9/27/05 | 2009

5 X 3 INCHES (12.7 X 7.6 CM)

Thrown and altered Laguna #250, dipped and brushed glaze, carved and pressed texture, propane fired, controlled cooling with water spray, reduction in wood shavings

PHOTO BY ARTIST

Gem Chang-Kue
Naked Raku Vase | 2009

5 X 6 INCHES (12.7 X 15.2 CM)

Wheel-thrown WSO, poured resist slip and glaze, burnished, beeswax polish, electric fired, propane fired, smoking for reduction, cone 016

PHOTO BY ARTIST

Leonid Siveriver
Ritual Vessel | 2007
22½ X 12½ X 8 INCHES (57.2 X 31.8 X 20.3 CM)
Slab-built, thrown, and altered raku clay with kyanite, brushed and sprayed glaze, gold and copper leaf slip, gas fired, controlled cooling, smoking for reduction
PHOTO BY WILLIAM VANDEVER

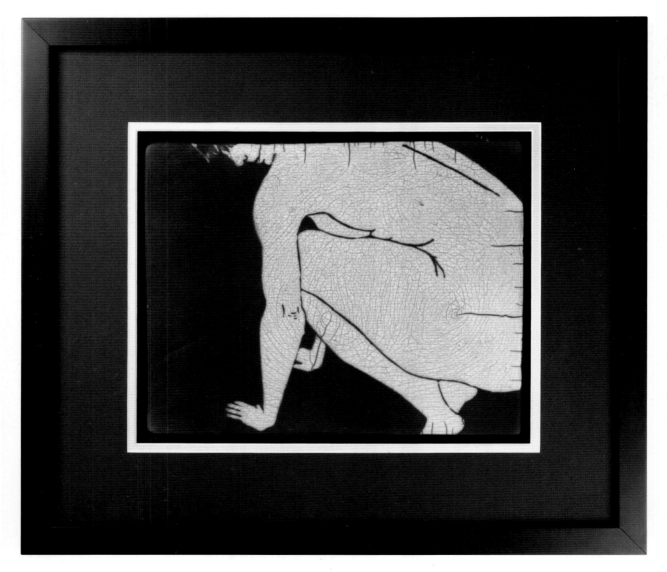

Shari Bray
Crouching | 2009
FRAMED: 18 X 20¼ INCHES (45.7 X 51.4 CM)
Slab-built Aardvark Raku white, brushed glaze, overglaze, raku fired, reduction in sawdust and newspaper
PHOTO BY KELLY MCLENDON

David Crane
Raku Box Group | 2007
TALLEST: 11 X 6 INCHES (27.9 X 15.2 CM)
Wheel-thrown and altered personal-recipe white raku, brushed glaze, rasped, burnished, multi-resist glazing, gas fired, smoking for reduction
PHOTO BY TIM BARNWELL

Linda Doherty
Earth and Pine Mongolian Pot | 2009
7½ X 7 X 7 INCHES (19.1 X 17.8 X 17.8 CM)
Wheel-thrown personal-recipe clay, pine needle stitched with waxed cotton, terra sigillata, gas fired, selective smoking for reduction with horsehair
PINE NEEDLE TRIM BY LYNNETTE GULLACKSON
PHOTO BY DENNIS DOHERTY

Janine Parent
Double Wall | 2008

10 X 8 INCHES (25.4 X 20.3 CM)

Wheel-thrown PSH Sheba Raku, brushed slip, poured glaze, naked raku, terra sigillata, electric fired, smoking for reduction

PHOTO BY GUY COUTURE

Alyson L. Murray
Kooza | 2007
7 X 11 X 3 INCHES (17.8 X 27.9 X 7.6 CM)
Hand-built, slab-built, and altered grogless raku clay, brushed glaze, faceted, stamped, gas fired, smoking for reduction, controlled reduction
PHOTO BY NAT CARON

Alma Moriah-Winik

Judith & Yuda | 2008

17 11/16 X 8 11/16 X 5 1/2 INCHES (44.9 X 22.1 X 14 CM)
Hand-built WBB Vingerling K129, sprayed glaze,
underglaze brushwork, gas fired, smoking for reduction

PHOTO BY ILAN AMICHAI

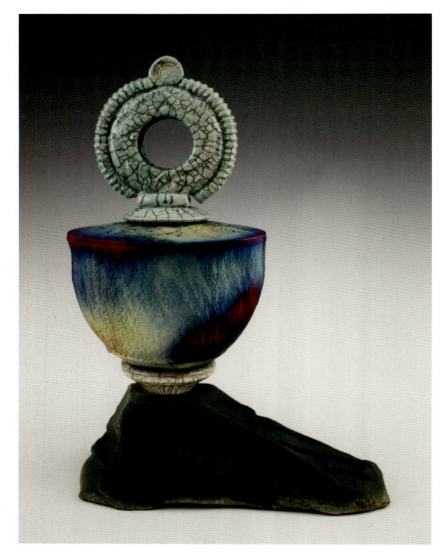

Gina Mars
Ritual Vessel | 2009
15 x 11 x 7 INCHES (38.1 x 27.9 x 17.8 CM)
Sculpted, thrown, and altered 239 Standard Raku Clay, sprayed and brushed glaze, stamped, carved, extruded, raku fired in propane kiln, alcohol reduction, reduction in sawdust
PHOTO BY ARTIST

Hasuyo V. Miller
Geisha | 2009
13 x 11 ½ x 5 INCHES (33 X 29.2 X 12.7 CM)
Slab-built white raku, brushed glaze, original stamp design, overglaze, propane fired, smoking for reduction, antique enamel, gold enhanced, cone 06
PHOTO BY ARTIST

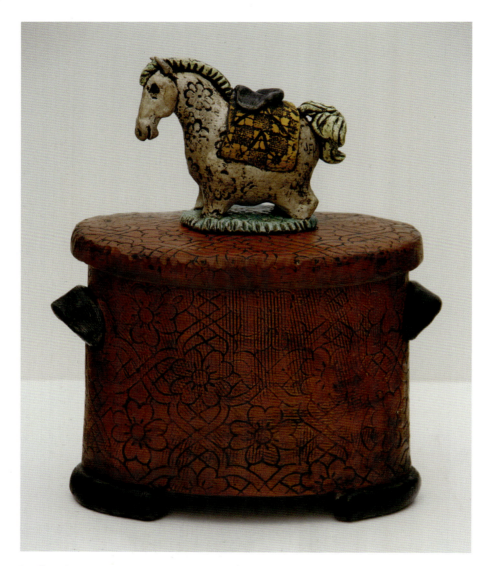

Jackie F. Harris
Untitled | 2009

10½ x 8½ x 6½ INCHES (26.7 x 21.6 x 16.5 CM)
Hand-built and slab-built Highwater Raku, terra sigillata, underglaze, glaze, patina, carved, stamped, gas fired, light reduction, selective smoking for reduction
PHOTO BY ARTIST

Marianne Kasparian
Steampunk | 2009
2 X 2 X 3/16 INCHES (5.1 X 5.1 X 0.5 CM)
Slab-built stoneware, brushed glaze, stamped,
propane fired, smoking for reduction
PHOTO BY DAVID ORR

Karen Anne van Barneveld-Price
World Peace Box | 2008
7 X 9 X 5 INCHES (17.8 X 22.9 X 12.7 CM)
Hand- and slab-built Soldate 60, brushed glaze, stamped, gas fired, smoking for reduction, cone 06
PHOTO BY ARTIST

Tom Mull
Moon Platter | 2007
13½ X 1½ INCHES (34.3 X 3.8 CM)
Deconstructed and reconstructed Clayplanet slabs on hump mold, brushed glaze, textured slab, gas fired, smoking for reduction, cone 05
PHOTO BY J. JONES

Truus Roest-Chapman
Sculpture | 2009
5½ X 11½ X 4 INCHES (14 X 29.2 X 10.2 CM)
Slab-built commercial raku, poured glaze, stamped, electric bisque fired, controlled cooling, smoking for reduction
PHOTO BY ARTIST

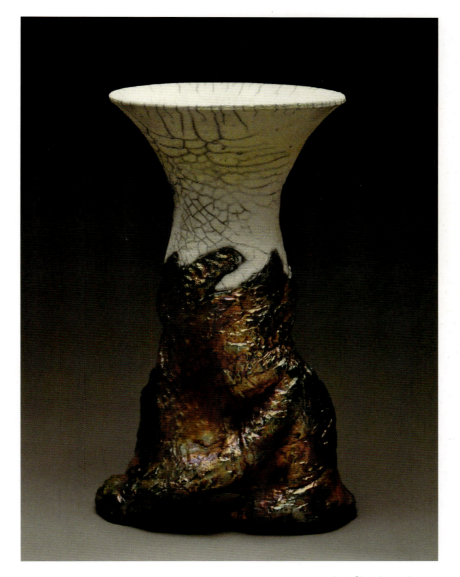

Leslie Ann Laws
Entwined | 2009
17 X 8 X 5 INCHES (43.2 X 20.3 X 12.7 CM)
Hand-built and wheel-thrown Balcones White Commercial Clay, brushed glaze, gas fired, smoking for reduction, cone 05
PHOTO BY DR. WILBURN LYNN LAWS

Shirley Clifford
Dharma Vessel | 2008

10 X 15 X 15 INCHES (25.4 X 38.1 X 38.1 CM)

Hand-built, wheel-thrown, and thrown and altered Tucker's 10-86 English Grolleg Porcelain and Porcelaneous Paper Clay, poured glaze, propane fired

PHOTO BY ARTIST

Robin Gail Beckett
Naked Raku Cauldron | 2009

4½ X 5½ INCHES (11.4 X 14 CM)

Thrown and altered Highwater Phoenix, dipped glaze, terra sigillata, naked raku, overglaze, gas fired, smoking for reduction, cone 04

PHOTO BY JAY WHITE

Jon Gariepy
Crackle Coupe | 2009

4 X 14 X 6 INCHES (10.2 X 35.6 X 15.2 CM)

Hand-built Imco Sculpture 412, brushed glaze, carved, overglazed, gas fired, smoking for reduction

PHOTOS BY CAROLYN CLOVER

Nici Ruggiero
Porcine | 2007
15¼ X 11 X 11 INCHES (38.7 X 27.9 X 27.9 CM)
Hand-built porcelain, unglazed, naked raku, electric and gas fired, smoking for reduction
PHOTO BY ARTIST

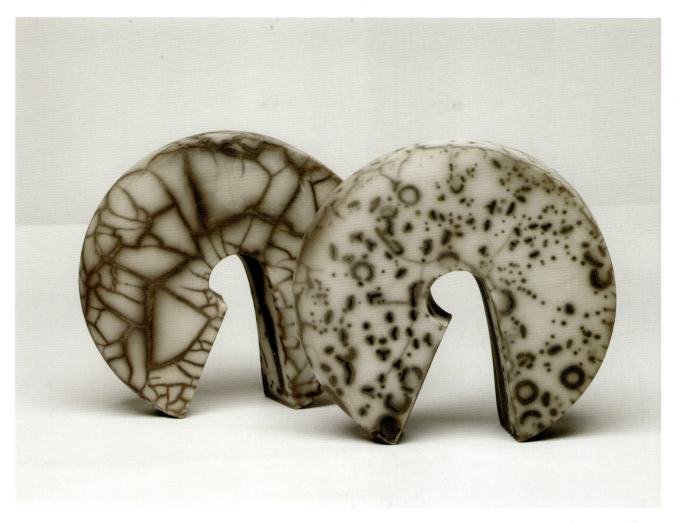

Sinéad Marie Glynn
Untitled Form III | 2009
EACH: 8 X 8½ X 2½ INCHES (20.3 X 21.6 X 6.4 CM)
Slip-cast white earthenware, casting slip CS60, resist under glaze, dipped and poured glaze, naked raku, gas fired, selective smoking for reduction
PHOTO BY GERRY MORGAN

JoAnn F. Axford
Columbine-Covered Jar | 2005
11 ½ X 8 ½ X 8 ½ INCHES (29.2 X 21.6 X 21.6 CM)
Wheel-thrown Laguna/Miller #66, brushed and poured glaze, sgraffito, gas fired, top hat raku, smoking for reduction
PHOTO BY ARTIST

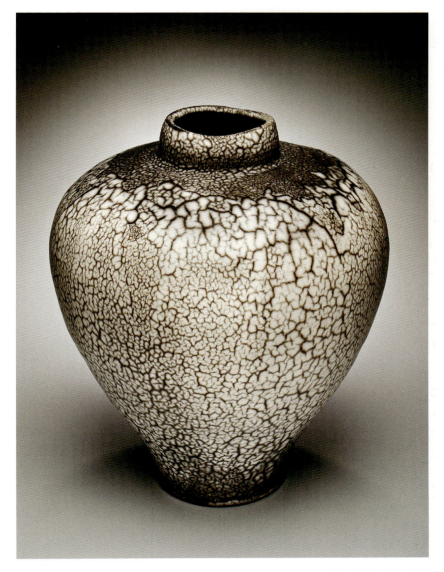

DeWitt Smith
Untitled | 2009

18 X 14 X 14 INCHES (45.7 X 35.6 X 35.6 CM)
Wheel-thrown personal-recipe clay, terra sigillata, gas fired,
smoking for reduction, bisque fired, cone 04, raku fired, cone 017

PHOTO BY WALKER MONTGOMERY

Nancy Zarbock
Autumn | 2009

14½ X 14½ INCHES (36.8 X 36.8 CM)

Press-molded and slab-built Standard Ceramic Raku Clay S295, brushed, dipped, sponged, poured, and splashed glaze, slip trailed, oxide wash, overglazed, stains, propane fired, smoking for reduction, cone 06

PHOTO BY WILLIAM L. ZARBOCK

Anthony E. Stellaccio
Hole in One | 2007

8 X 13 X 5 INCHES (20.3 X 33 X 12.7 CM)

Slab-built commercial earthenware, brushed glaze, wood fired, smoking for reduction

PHOTO BY ARTIST

Lambeth Walker Marshall
Untitled Raku Globe | 2009
12 INCHES (30.5 CM) IN DIAMETER
Wheel-thrown Highwater Raku, sprayed glaze, underglaze, overglazed, raku top hat propane fired, selective smoking for reduction
PHOTO BY ARTIST

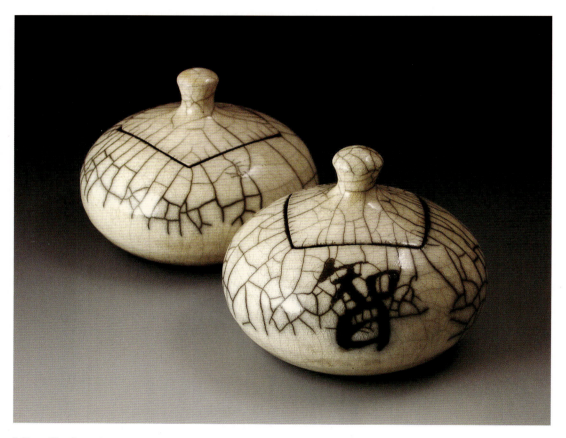

Miya Endo
Untitled | 2009

EACH: 3½ X 3 X 3 INCHES (8.9 X 7.6 X 7.6 CM)
Wheel-thrown Laguna Half-and-Half Commercial Clay, dipped glaze, wax resist, gas fired, controlled cooling, smoking for reduction, cone 06
PHOTO BY ARTIST

Josse Davis
Kings Arms (Pub) II | 2007
13 INCHES (33 CM) IN DIAMETER
Wheel-thrown personal-recipe clay, brushed glaze,
transparent glaze, gas fired, smoking for reduction
PHOTO BY ARTIST

Irina Clopatofsky Velasco
Forest Night | 2008
8¾ X 9½ X 1½ INCHES (22.2 X 24.1 X 3.8 CM)
Hand-built, slab-built, and wheel-thrown Miller Clay #200, brushed glaze, carved, gas fired, reduction, cooled with water
PHOTO BY RYAN FLATHAU

Teri Hannigan
Pillow Pot | 2008

5 X 8 X 7 INCHES (12.7 X 20.3 X 17.8 CM)
Altered and slab-built Laguna B-Mix, sprayed and brushed glazes, carved, gas fired, no-reduction air cooling

PHOTO BY ANTHONY CUNHA

Ellen Silberlicht
Elephant Twist | 2009
13 x 9 x 9 INCHES (33 X 22.9 X 22.9 CM)
Wheel-thrown and hand-built Standard #239, brushed glaze, wax resist, raku fired gas, sawdust for reduction
PHOTO BY ARTIST

Iris Minc
Pillow Form Turquoise Raku Bottle | 2006

8½ X 5 X 2½ INCHES (21.6 X 12.7 X 6.4 CM)

Slab-built personal-recipe clay, brushed and dipped glaze, wax resist, gas fired, smoking for reduction, cone 05

PHOTO BY JOHN POLAK

Liz de Beer
Porcupine Jar | 2009

11 X 7 X 7 INCHES (27.9 X 17.8 X 17.8 CM)

Wheel-thrown industrial raku, brushed glaze, oxide wash, gas fired, smoking for reduction

PHOTO BY JAN DE BEER

Nancy Louise Cramer
Spirit Within | 2007
10 X 3½ INCHES (27.9 X 8.9 CM)
Hand-built raku, brushed glaze, stamped, woven, gas fired, smoking for reduction
PHOTO BY ARTIST

Valerie Yardley
Family | 2009
10 X 9 X 8 INCHES (25.4 X 22.9 X 20.3 CM)
Hand-built raku, brushed glaze, tintype photographs edged in copper, gas fired, selective smoking for reduction
PHOTO BY PETER LESTER

Rose Kadera Vastila
Watchers | 2006
13 X 10 X 6 INCHES (33 X 25.4 X 15.2 CM)
Hand and slab-built commercial raku clay, dipped glaze, modeled, gas fired, smoking for reduction in sawdust
PHOTO BY JEFF FREY & ASSOCIATES

Carla Horowitz
Untitled | 2007

5½ X 7½ X 7½ INCHES (14 X 19.1 X 19.1 CM)
Thrown, cut, and coiled clay, brushed glaze, splattered halo slip, selective smoking for reduction
PHOTO BY GERALD SLOTA

Don Hall
Raku Gadget | 2009
18 X 15 X 6 INCHES (45.7 X 38.1 X 15.2 CM)
Slab-built and wheel-thrown Orion Stout/Clay Planet Commercial Clay, brushed glaze, stamped, rolled texture, recycled cooking oil, smoking for reduction in newspaper, cone 07
PHOTO BY ARTIST

Liz Pasenow
Bowl with Stretched Rim Addition | 2008
6 X 13 X 5 INCHES (15.2 X 33 X 12.7 CM)
Wheel-thrown and stretched Sheba Raku, sprayed glaze, propane fired, smoking for reduction
PHOTO BY SHEILA CLENNELL

Hongwei Li
Self-Portrait #9 | 2006
20 X 43 X 18 INCHES (50.8 X 109.2 X 45.7 CM)
Slab-built earthenware, brushed glaze,
gas fired, smoking for reduction, cone 06
PHOTO BY ARTIST

Carole Fleischman
Nobel Gold Whiskers—Saynomore | 2009
8¾ X 14¾ X 4¾ INCHES (22.2 X 37.5 X 12.1 CM)
Sculpted, hand-, and slab-built white stoneware, brushed and poured glaze, underglaze, coated wire whiskers, electric and raku fired, pulled, sprayed with alcohol, reduction in can, burped to introduce oxygen
PHOTO BY ARTIST

Nesrin During
Untitled | 2007
4¹¹⁄₁₆ X 5⅛ INCHES (12 X 13 CM)
Hand-built Westerwalder Clay, poured glaze, overglazed, wood fired, smoking for reduction
PHOTO BY STEFAN DURING

Rita Ruth Cockrell
Extruded Man | 2007
10 X 8 X 2½ INCHES (25.4 X 20.3 X 6.4 CM)
Extruded and sculpted Highwater Brownstone Clay, brushed glaze, carved, gas fired, quick cooling in water, smoking for reduction
PHOTO BY ARTIST

Susan Kirchmer
Black Pine, Bonsai | 2008
19 X 8 INCHES (48.3 X 20.3 CM)
Wheel-thrown Bruce's White Clay, brushed stain and glazes, hand carved, raku fired, cone 06
PHOTO BY JIM KIRCHMER

Paul Carl Estes
Untitled | 2009
6 X 5¼ X 5¼ INCHES (15.2 X 13.3 X 13.3 CM)
Hand-built and wheel-thrown Amaco Raku No. 27, brushed glaze, gas fired, smoking for reduction, air cooling
PHOTO BY ARTIST

Jana Diedrich
Copper Fish | 2008
8 X 12 X 4 INCHES (20.3 X 30.5 X 10.2 CM)
Hand-built Kyan raku, sprayed glaze, carved, stamped, gas fired, selective smoking for reduction
PHOTO BY ARTIST

Karen A. Case
Red Bird Whistle | 2009
2 X 4 X 2 INCHES (5.1 X 10.2 X 5.1 CM)
Hand-built Laguna Porcelain, brushed glaze, gas fired, newspaper reduction, cone 06
PHOTO BY ARTIST

Marvin Sweet
Bisnaga 11 | 2009
11 ½ x 10 x 10 INCHES (29.2 x 25.4 x 25.4 CM)
Hand-built and slab-built personal-recipe clay, sprayed glaze, paint, non-fired, gas fired, smoking for reduction
PHOTO BY LISA NUGENT

Vicki Rapport Paulet
Black Hole | 2005

8 X 10½ INCHES (20.3 X 26.7 CM)

Hand-built and wheel-thrown raku/white stoneware slip, brushed glaze, gas fired, smoking for reduction

PHOTO BY EDDIE ING

Carol Rossman
Barcelona Series #1 | 2007

5½ X 7½ INCHES (14 X 19.1 CM)

Wheel-thrown Michael Sheba Raku, brushed and sprayed glazes, burnished terra sigillata, glazes, oxides, tapes removed, propane fired, reduction in sawdust and newspaper, quick re-oxidation, covered and left until cool, cone 08

PHOTO BY MICHAEL DISMATSEK

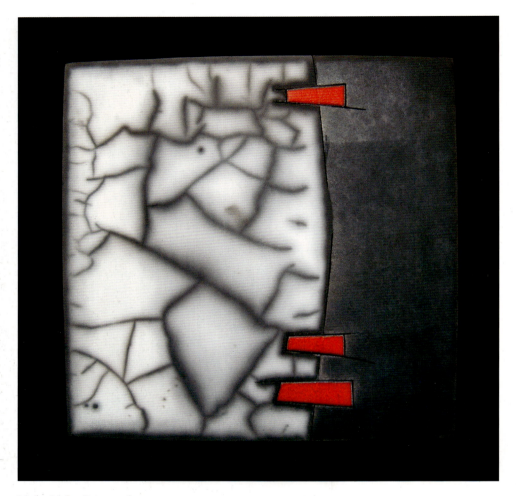

Yola Vale Resende
Untitled | 2007
1 X 12 X 12 INCHES (2.5 X 30.5 X 30.5 CM)
Hand-built CH-B, Vicente Diez commercial clay, brushed glaze, carved, overglaze, terra sigillata, gas fired, smoking for reduction
PHOTO BY ARTIST

Linda Hansen Mau
Memories of Arizona | 2005
8 X 8 X 8 INCHES (20.3 X 20.3 X 20.3 CM)
Wheel-thrown B-Mix with grog, brushed glaze over terra sigillata, penciled image, painted, gas fired, smoking for reduction in newspaper, slow cooling, cone 06
PHOTO BY ARTIST

Simcha Even-Chen
A Moment Before . . . | 2009
4½ X 12 X 9⅜ INCHES (11.4 X 30.5 X 23.8 CM)
Slab-built Vingerling K129 and K130, naked raku,
masking technique, gas fired, quick smoking
PHOTO BY ILAN AMIHAI

Emma Johnstone
Teardrop Segment | 2006

7 X 5½ X 5½ INCHES (17.8 X 14 X 14 CM)

Slab-built, thrown, and altered Scarva Professional White Raku, brushed glaze, naked raku, burnished, waxed, gas fired, smoking for reduction

PHOTO BY JAMES WADDELL

Jo-Ann Gartner
Ribbon and Beads Box | 2007

7½ X 7 X 7 INCHES (19.1 X 17.8 X 17.8 CM)

Slab-built Standard Raku 239, tar paper, brushed glaze, overglazed beads, gas fired, ferric chloride fumed, smoking for reduction

PHOTO BY THOMAS DECKER

Audrey Nimmo
Cats of Symi, Greece | 2008
10 X 8 X 2 INCHES (25.4 X 20.3 X 5.1 CM)
Relief-sculpted, hand-built, and slab-built raku, brushed glaze, carved, underglaze brushwork, propane fired, selective smoking for reduction
PHOTO BY SHEILA CLENNELL

Elaine Klaasen Kryger
Turquoise Vase | 2009
16 X 32 INCHES (40.6 X 81.3 CM)
Wheel-thrown Trinity Red Stoneware, brushed glaze, gas fired, selective smoking for reduction
PHOTO BY ROSS SKEEGAN

Marc Leuthold
Twins | 2008

2 X 7 X 3 INCHES (5.1 X 17.8 X 7.6 CM)

Wheel-thrown and carved porcelain, no glaze plus oxides, oil fired raku, smoking for reduction, cone 04

PHOTO BY EVA HEYD

Jane McDonald
Blood Vessel | 2008

15 X 10 X 11 INCHES (38.1 X 25.4 X 27.9 CM)

Slab-built stoneware, brushed and poured glaze, textured, stretched, low-fire overglaze, propane fired in raku kiln, controlled cooling, reduction with newsprint

PHOTO BY JOSEPH MCDONALD

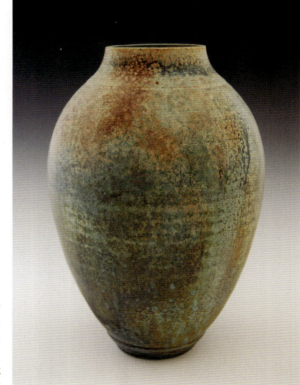

Joseph J. Battiato
Lori Luster Vase | 2009

14 X 9 INCHES (35.6 X 22.9 CM)

Wheel-thrown Clay Planet Orion Stout, sprayed glaze, gas fired, quick smoking

PHOTO BY ARTIST

Ilena Finocchi
Binding Thoughts | 2006
8 X 7½ X 9 INCHES (20.3 X 19.1 X 22.9 CM)
Press-molded and altered ABFSL, brushed terra sigillata,
burnished, carved, gas fired, new sawdust, smoking for reduction
PHOTO BY ARTIST

Beth R. Kamhi
Secret Life of . . . Memories | 2008
18 X 6 X 8 INCHES (45.7 X 15.2 X 20.3 CM)
Raku, brushed glaze, carved, post-fire water slide decals, forged steel branches and nest, electric and gas fired, quick cooling in water, smoking for reduction
PHOTO BY ARTIST

Deborah Johnston
Untitled | 2008
5 X 7 INCHES (12.7 X 17.7 CM)
Hand-built stoneware, brushed glaze, carved, gas fired, quick smoking
PHOTO BY ARTIST

Judy Henderson
Thinking Inside the Box | 2007

4 X 4 X 13 INCHES (10.2 X 10.2 X 33 CM)

Slab-built Laguna W50, brushed glazes, stamped, textured, gas-fired raku, slightly cooled, heavily smoked in metal trash can, cone 06

PHOTO BY LARRY PENNINGTON

Jesse Showalter
Deep Reflection | 2009
9 X 12 INCHES (22.9 X 30.5 CM)
Slab press-molded stoneware with grog added, burnished, slip, bisqueware, slip resist, selective smoking for reduction, 1832°F (1000°C)
PHOTO BY KARA TAYLOR

Ritsuko Moore
Open-Shaped Bowl | 2009
3½ X 15 X 15 INCHES (8.9 X 38.1 X 38.1 CM)
Wheel-thrown raku clay, brushed glaze, taping, gas fired, quick smoking
PHOTO BY ARTIST

Joan A. Powell
Watermarks Naked Raku | 2007

6 X 6 X 6 INCHES (15.2 X 15.2 X 15.2 CM)

Wheel-thrown and altered porcelain, poured slip and glaze, naked raku, gas fired, smoking for reduction, 1430°F (777°C)

PHOTO BY JON KOCH

Jim Connell
Red Carved Lidded Jar | 2005

13 X 13 X 13 INCHES (33 X 33 X 33 CM)

Thrown, paddled, and carved stoneware/raku, sprayed glaze, electric fired, quick smoking, smoking for reduction, cone 06

PHOTO BY ARTIST

Candone Marie Wharton
Plato Rojo | 2007
2 X 17 X 17 INCHES (5.1 X 43.2 X 43.2 CM)
Hand-built, slab-built, and carved Highwater Phoenix, dipped glaze, carved, slip trailed, luster, electric fired, gas fired, quick cooling in water, quick smoking, heavy reduction
PHOTO BY JERRY ANTHONY

Marianne G. Tebbens
Serenity | 2006
8 X 12 X 12 INCHES (20.3 X 30.5 X 30.5 CM)
Relief sculpted and slab-built Standard Raku, poured glaze, propane fired, smoking for reduction
PHOTO BY JOHN J. CARLANO

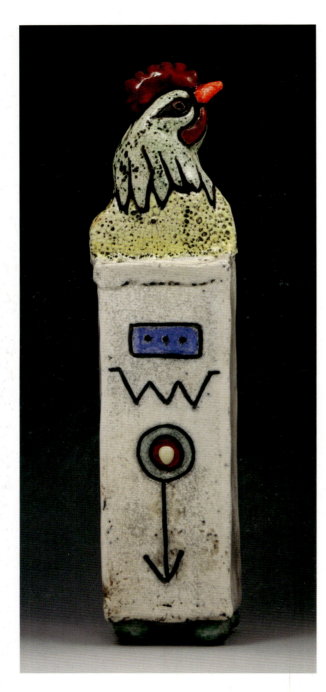

Betsy Cox
Rooster Shrine #9 Redux | 2008
14 X 4 X 4 INCHES (35.6 X 10.2 X 10.2 CM)
Press-molded, hand-built, and slab-built
Laguna WS0, brushed glaze, carved,
sgraffito, gas fired, smoking for reduction
PHOTO BY ARTIST

Julie C. Hilliard
Untitled | 2007
9 X 11 ½ X 3 INCHES (22.9 X 29.2 X 7.6 CM)
Hand-built and slab-built Highwater Raku, brushed glazes, overglaze luster, gas fired, smoking for reduction, newspaper combustible
PHOTO BY WALKER MONTGOMERY

Barbara Harnack
Angel in My House | 2009
21 X 13 X 12 INCHES (53.3 X 33 X 30.5 CM)
Slab-built Laguna Big White Stoneware, brushed glaze, underglaze brushwork, overglazed, incised, gas fired, smoking for reduction in straw
PHOTO BY ARTIST

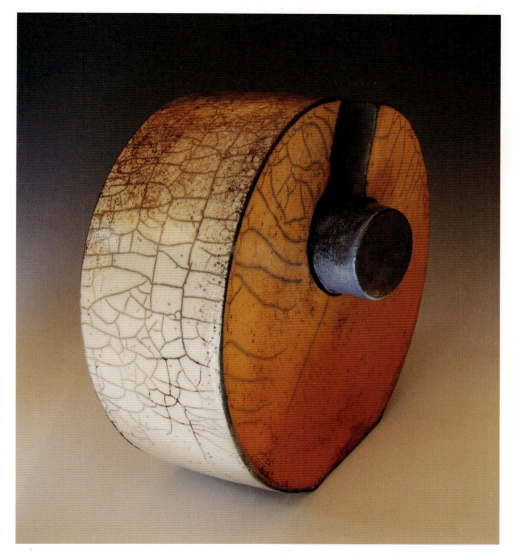

Michael Lancaster
Tension | 2009
17 X 18 X 12 INCHES (43.2 X 45.7 X 30.5 CM)
Thrown, altered, and assembled Laguna Big White
Stoneware, brushed glaze, underglaze brushwork, overglaze,
gas fired, smoking for reduction in straw
PHOTO BY ARTIST

Don Fritz
Atomic Iron | 2009
20 X 12 X 9 INCHES (50.8 X 30.5 X 22.9 CM)
Hand-built and slab-built sculpture raku, brushed glaze, underglaze brushwork, overglazed, gas fired, smoking for reduction, cone 06
PHOTO BY R.R. JONES

Gennady Roitich
Ceramotecton | 2005
LARGEST: 30 X 55 X 8 INCHES (76.2 X 139.7 X 20.3 CM)
Hand-built stoneware, brushed and splashed glaze, carved, gas fired, quick cooling in water, smoking for reduction
PHOTO BY ILAN AMICHAY

Sam Scott
Squares and Pours Vase | 2009
9 X 6 X 6 INCHES (22.9 X 15.2 X 15.2 CM)
Wheel-thrown Scott Stoneware, poured, masked, propane fired, smoking for reduction with controlled cooling, cone 06
PHOTO BY ARTIST

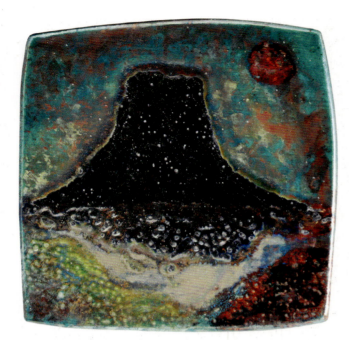

George Tomkins
Yuma Sunset #10 | 2009
12 x 12 x 1½ INCHES (30.5 X 30.5 X 3.8 CM)
Slab and wheel-thrown Laguna Big White, brushed glaze, gas-fired raku, selective smoking for reduction
PHOTO BY ARTIST

Cathryn R. Hudin
At Peace | 2006
14 x 12 x 2 INCHES (35.6 X 30.5 X 5.1 CM)
Slab-built Raku-C, brushed and poured glaze, stamped, waxed, incised, gas fired, controlled cooling, smoking for reduction
PHOTO BY ARTIST

Lisa Merida-Paytes
Fish in Rock | 2007

20 X 31 X 18 INCHES (50.8 X 78.7 X 45.7 CM)

Press-molded, relief-sculpted, hand-built, and slab-built Columbus Raku, brushed glaze, carved, stamped, overglazed, gas fired, controlled cooling, selective smoking for reduction, cone 05

PHOTO BY JAY BACHEMIN

Candy Casarella
Firewater | 2008

10 x 3½ x 3½ INCHES (25.4 X 8.9 X 8.9 CM)
Wheel-thrown Kickwheel Raku KPS, dipped and sprayed glaze, gas-fired raku, smoking for reduction
PHOTO BY PEGGY ALBERS

Lisa Hueil Conner
Mermaid | 2006
14 X 17 X 6 INCHES (35.6 X 43.2 X 15.2 CM)
Hand-built, slab-built, carved, and sculpted Standard 295 Raku, brushed and poured glaze, carved, overglazed, underglaze wash, gas fired, quick cooling in water, smoking for reduction
PHOTO BY JAY BACHEMIN

500 RAKU

William R. Schran
Four-Leg Vessel | 2008
8 X 5 X 5 INCHES (20.3 X 12.7 X 12.7 CM)
Wheel-thrown and hand-built Soldate 60, sprayed glaze, impressed, gas fired, smoking for reduction
PHOTO BY ARTIST

Anne Louise Armstrong
Reliquary | 2009
24 X 9 INCHES (61 X 22.9 CM)
Wheel-thrown Sheba Raku, no glaze, sprayed with ferric chloride, applied horsehair, 1400°F (760°C), gas fired, no-reduction air cooling
PHOTO BY ARTIST

Alistair Danhieux
Grande Disque | 2009
5½ X 16 INCHES (14 X 40.6 CM)
Wheel-thrown and assembled Fuchs-K129, slip, glaze,
naked raku, sgraffito, gas fired, smoking for reduction
PHOTO BY HERVÉ JÉZÉQUEL

Kathy Phelps
Black and White | 2008
5¾ X 4¼ X 4¼ INCHES (14.6 X 10.8 X 10.8 CM)
Wheel-thrown white stoneware, splashed glaze, terra sigillata, gas fired, smoking for reduction
PHOTO BY WALKER MONTGOMERY

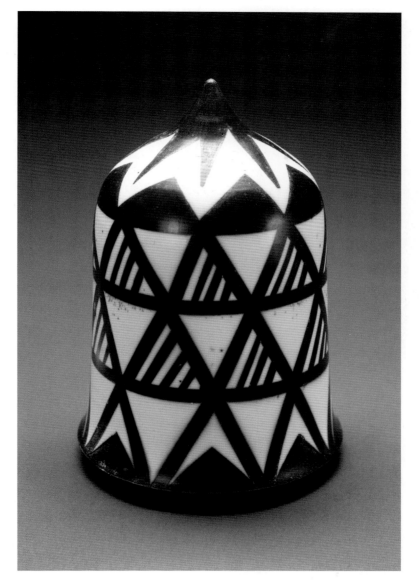

Pia Sillem
Round and Round | 2009
8¼ X 5½ INCHES (21 X 14 CM)
Wheel-thrown 555, naked raku, gas fired, smoking for reduction
PHOTO BY MICHAEL O'SHEA

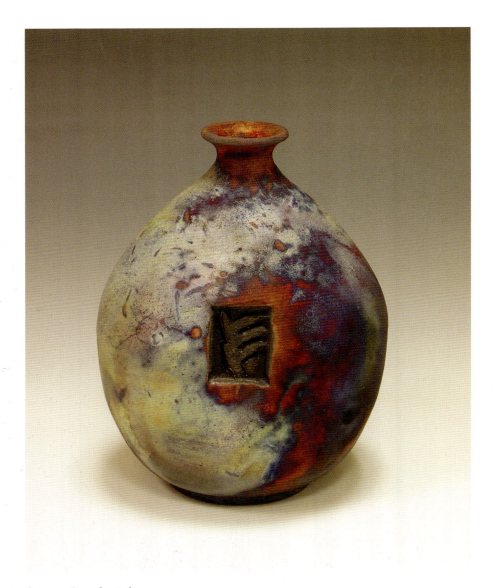

Susan Broderick
Raku-Fired Stamped Bottle | 2007
7 X 3½ INCHES (17.8 X 8.9 CM)
Wheel-thrown and pressed Standard Raku 239, brushed glaze, gas-fired raku, selective smoking for reduction
PHOTO BY CHRIS VIVAS

Rhea Moss

Yesterday's Treasures | 2007

5 X 4¼ INCHES (12.7 X 10.8 CM)

Wheel-thrown stoneware with grog, dipped glaze, carved, gas fired, smoking for reduction, 1832° F (1000°C)

PHOTO BY KARA TAYLOR

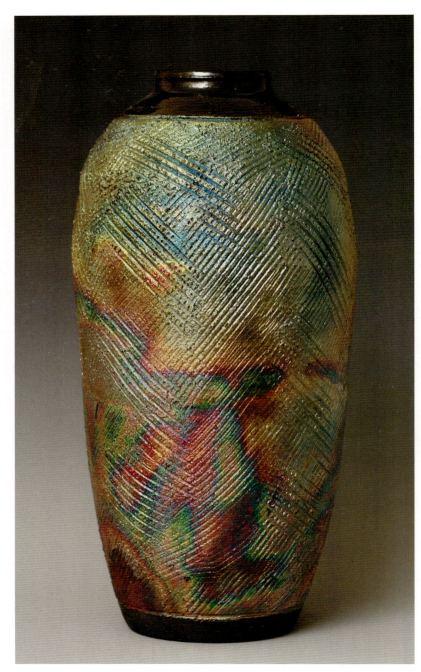

Cynthia L. Prince
Untitled | 2007

12½ x 6½ x 6½ INCHES (31.8 x 16.5 x 16.5 CM)
Wheel-thrown raku 239, brushed glaze, carved, gas fired, smoking for reduction
PHOTO BY JESSICA SCHEUFLER

Bob Miranti
Two Fancy Ladies Walking | 2007
TALLEST: 10 X 4 X 4 INCHES (25.4 X 10.2 X 10.2 CM)
Altered and extruded stoneware, poured glaze, stains, gas fired, smoking for reduction
PHOTO BY ARTIST

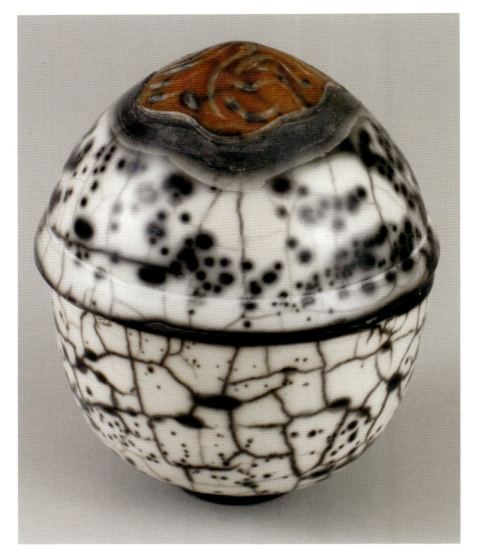

Alison Lauriat
Egg-Shaped Container | 2009
15 X 6 INCHES (38.1 X 15.2 CM)
Wheel-thrown studio porcelain, naked raku slip, dipped glaze, carved, terra sigillata, polished, gas fired, smoked with combustibles, cooling in water
PHOTO BY RONNIE GOULD

Judy Geerts
Wild Bird | 2008
30 X 22 X 17 INCHES (76.2 X 55.9 X 43.2 CM)
Hand-built, slab-built, and pinched Great Lakes Smooth Raku, brushed and sprayed glaze, carved, stamped, non-ceramic, electric and gas fired, controlled cooling

PHOTO BY PAT CHAMBERS

Dave Deal
Boni Deal
Heron/Moon Wall Platter | 2008
24 X 24 X 3 INCHES (61 X 61 X 7.6 CM)
Wheel-thrown Laguna Soldate 30, sprayed and brush-textured glaze, incised, propane fired, in-kiln reduction, post-kiln smoking for reduction, slow cooling in barrel
PHOTO BY BONNIE DUNGAN

Frances Neish
Untitled | 2009
3 X 10¾ INCHES (7.6 X 27.3 CM)
Wheel-thrown Thompson Raku, poured glaze, sgraffito, electric fired, propane fired, smoking for reduction
PHOTO BY ARTIST

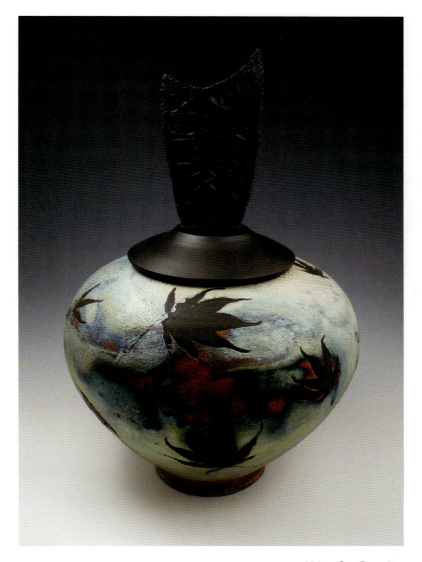

Wanda Garrity
Sailing through Fall | 2009
18 × 11 × 11 INCHES (45.7 × 27.9 × 27.9 CM)
Wheel-thrown and slab-built Hutchens Raku, brushed glaze, resist, stamped, painted, electric fired, raku fired, reduction in trashcan with newspaper, 1850°F (1010°C)
PHOTO BY ARTIST

Merla Frazey-Jordan
The Storm | 2005

10½ X 14 X ¾ INCHES (26.7 X 35.6 X 1.9 CM)
Relief-sculpted and slab-built high-fire, brushed glaze, carved, electric fired, gas fired, reduction in pine needles
PHOTO BY ARTIST

Nathan C. Webb
Plate | 2007

8 X 8 X 2½ INCHES (20.3 X 20.3 X 6.4 CM)
Slab-built personal-recipe clay, brushed and poured glaze, burnished terra sigillata, incised through glaze resist, gas fired, cone 04

PHOTO BY BECCA VAN FLEET

Tracey Broome
Green Pear with Metal Stand | 2009
4 X 6 INCHES (10.2 X 15.2 CM)
Hand-built clay, brushed glaze, gas fired,
1900°F (1038°C), no-reduction air cooling
PHOTO BY GERRY BROOME

Krysia St. Clair
Cracked Earth | 2009
14 X 10 INCHES (35.6 X 25.4 CM)
Press-molded Walker No. 10 porcelaneous clay, poured glaze,
dry lithium glazed. gas fired, heavy reduction in straw
PHOTO BY ARTIST

Linda Harris
Fish | 2008
11 X 13 X 8 INCHES (27.9 X 33 X 20.3 CM)
Hand-built Tucker's Raku-White Sculpture Clay, brushed glaze, carved, gas fired, controlled cooling, smoking for reduction
PHOTO BY ARTIST

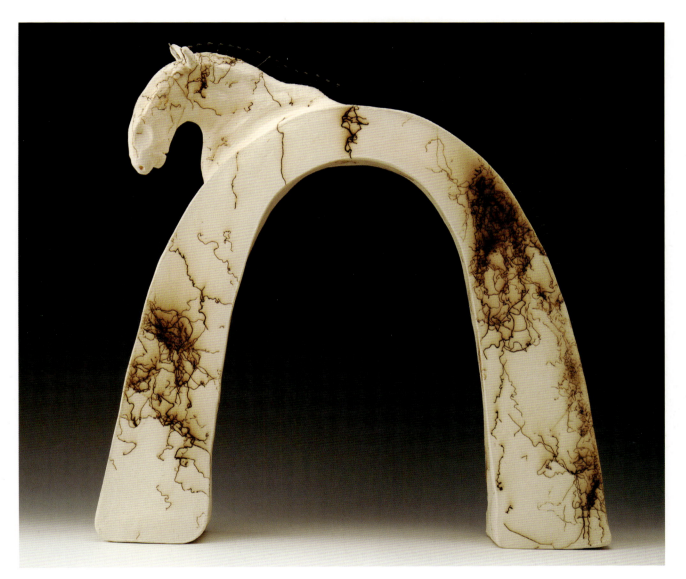

Richard T. Hess
Poetry in Motion | 2009
20 x 19 x 3 INCHES (50.8 x 48.3 x 7.6 CM)
Slab-constructed and sculpted Armadillo Raku, horsehair applied to hot surface, 1200°F (649°C), horseshoe nails, greenware, fired
PHOTO BY ROM WELBORN

Ruth E. Allan
Firebird #17 | 2007

13 X 10 INCHES (33 X 25.4 CM)

Relief-sculpted, wheel-thrown, and hand carved stoneware, poured glaze, carved, gas fired, quick cooling in water, smoking for reduction, cone 04

PHOTO BY ARTIST

Gino Parisi
Egg Shell | 2009

3 X 3¾ INCHES (7.6 X 9.5 CM)

Wheel-thrown Laguna Windsor Porcelain, poured glaze, gas fired, selective smoking for reduction

PHOTO BY BRUCE DOUGLAS

Ann Testa
Pears on a Tray | 2008

EACH: 5 X 4 INCHES (12.7 X 10.1 CM) EACH
Wheel-thrown and altered East Bay Clay Smooth
Raku, brushed glaze, gas fired, ferric oxide, smoked

PHOTO BY HAP SAKWA

E. Tyler Burton
Kansha | 2008
14 X 4 X 4 INCHES (35.6 X 10.2 X 10.2 CM)
Hand-built B-Mix and paper clay, brushed glaze, gas-fired raku, smoking for reduction in straw and leaves
PHOTO BY ARTIST

Mirtha Aertker
Heart Disk | 2009
16 X 10 X 8 INCHES (40.6 X 25.4 X 20.3 CM)
Wheel-thrown and altered porcelain, brushed glaze, carved, stamped, gas fired, controlled cooling, smoking for reduction, selective smoking
PHOTO BY ARTIST

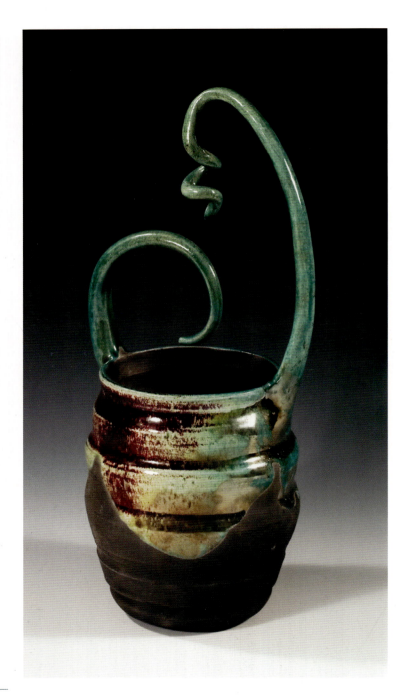

Jamie Lynn Cream
Untitled | 2008
14 X 6 INCHES (35.6 X 15.2 CM)
Wheel-thrown and hand-built Ceramic Supply Raku, poured glaze, overglazed, gas fired, smoking for reduction, quick cooling in water, cone 05
PHOTO BY KELLY MULLIGAN

Cher Shackleton
Raku Vase | 2009
7½ X 2⅜ X 2⅜ INCHES (19.1 X 6 X 6 CM)
Extruded and altered Clayworks LGH, brushed glaze, wood fired, smoking for reduction
PHOTO BY ARTIST

Jill Helen Getzan
Fire Dish | 2009

5 X 8 X 8 INCHES (12.7 X 20.3 X 20.3 CM)

Slab-built Laguna Soldate 60, brushed glaze, stamped, gas fired, smoking for reduction, cone 06

PHOTO BY ARTIST

Tripti Yoganathan
It's All About Me | 2007

5 X 6 X 6 INCHES (12.7 X 15.2 X 15.2 CM)

Thrown and altered raku, dipped glaze, gas-fired raku, smoking for reduction

PHOTO BY WALKER P. MONTGOMERY

Jon Gariepy
Self Portrait | 2007
8 X 18 X 6 INCHES (20.3 X 45.7 X 15.2 CM)
Hand-built Imco Sculpture 412, brushed glaze, carved, stamped, sgraffito, underglaze brushwork, overglazed, paint/non-ceramic/non-fired, gas fired, smoking for reduction

PHOTO BY CAROLYN CLOVER

Suzanne Shelley
Assembled 5 | 2006
10 X 6 X 3 INCHES (25.4 X 15.2 X 7.6 CM)
Slab-built paper clay, brushed glaze, mixed-media post-firing, gas fired, smoking in sawdust, quick cooling
PHOTO BY ARTIST

Priya Tambe
Thinking | 2009
3 X 4 X 3½ INCHES (7.6 X 10.2 X 8.9 CM)
Hand-built Standard 239, brushed glaze,
electric fired, gas fired, controlled cooling
PHOTO BY LOREN MARON

Susan Wortman
Winged Woman | 2007

7½ X 3 X 2½ INCHES (19.1 X 7.6 X 6.4 CM)

Hand-built porcelain, dipped glaze, stamped, electric fired, smoking for reduction, raku

PHOTO BY GEORGIA TENORE

Laura Peters
Untitled | 2008

11½ X 5½ X 4½ INCHES (29.2 X 14 X 11.4 CM)

Slab-built white rose, brushed glaze, underglaze brushwork, raku fired, quick smoking, cone 6

PHOTO BY LINDA STEPHENS

James Bassett
Two Birds | 2009
EACH: 6 X 9 X 5 INCHES (15.2 X 22.9 X 12.7 CM)
Press-molded and slab-built Scava Earthstone, dipped glaze, wax resist, electric fired, propane fired, air cooling, smoking in hardwood shavings, quenching in water
PHOTO BY JOHN MATHIESON

Sylvia Shiu-Wai McGourlick
Amphora II | 2009
8 X 7 X 7 INCHES (20.3 X 17.8 X 17.8 CM)
Wheel-thrown Laguna Clay WSO, dipped and brushed glaze, gas fired, smoking for reduction
PHOTO BY BRIAN KYLE

Kenneth Michael Wallace
Naked Raku Flying Saucer | 2006
6½ X 11 X 11 INCHES (16.5 X 27.9 X 27.9 CM)
Wheel-thrown Clay Planet Bravo Buff, splashed glaze, gas fired, smoking for reduction
PHOTO BY ARTIST

Sheldon Ganstrom
Altar | 2009
24 X 21 X 18 INCHES (61 X 53.3 X 45.7 CM)

Slab-built, press-molded, and hand-built white stoneware with kyanite, brushed glazes and engobes, silver nitrate overglaze, electric fired, cooled, heavy multi-can reduction, cone 07

PHOTOS BY ARTIST

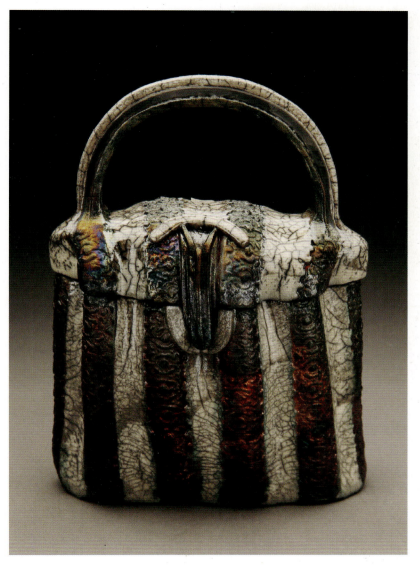

Bonnie Rae Shaver
Copper and White Purse | 2007
11 X 8 X 4½ INCHES (27.9 X 20.3 X 11.4 CM)
Slab-built white stoneware, brushed glaze, stamped, stretched,
gas fired, smoking for reduction, quick cooling in water
PHOTO BY LOREN MARON

Mary Carolyn Obodzinski
Three Raku Vessels | 2008
TALLEST: 12 X 13 X 4 INCHES (30.5 X 33 X 10.2 CM)
Hand-built, slab-built, and hand-textured commercial raku clay, brushed glaze, stamped, gas fired, controlled cooling in a lidded can with newspaper, heavy reduction, cone 06
PHOTO BY DAVID A. RENCH

John P. Armstrong
Dimple Raku Bowl | 2009

6 X 6 X 6 INCHES (15.2 X 15.2 X 15.2 CM)
Thrown and altered white clay, dipped glaze, gas fired, smoking for reduction
PHOTO BY ARTIST

Jo-Michele Boyer-Sebern
Horses Series | 2009

4½ X 4½ X 3 INCHES (11.4 X 11.4 X 7.6 CM)
Wheel-thrown stoneware, brushed iron oxide glaze, gas fired, smoking for reduction, cone 06
PHOTO BY LARRY HOAGLAND

Gerry Dinnen
Untitled | 2007
10 X 7 X 3 INCHES (25.4 X 17.8 X 7.6 CM)
Slab-built Standard Ceramics 239, brushed glaze, stenciled, gas-fired raku, smoking for reduction
PHOTO BY JOSEPH DELPHIA

Dan Hawkins
Artifact #2 | 2009
18 X 18 X 3 INCHES (45.7 X 45.7 X 7.6 CM)
Slab-built paper clay, brushed glaze, mixed media applied post-firing,
electric fired, heavy reduction, bisque, cone 04, glaze, cone 06
PHOTO BY ARTIST

Patricia Cohen
Emergence | 2009

12½ X 8½ X 8½ INCHES (31.8 X 21.6 X 21.6 CM)

Hand-built, drape molded, and coiled New Mexico Raku, brushed glaze, string trailed, overglazed, electric fired, smoking for reduction, cone 06, wood, waxed cotton string, metal base

PHOTO BY MARGOT GEIST

Sharon Bartmann
Oil Cans 2 | 2007
13½ X 7½ X 3½ INCHES (34.3 X 19.1 X 8.9 CM)
Hand-built raku clay, brushed glaze, decal, overglazed, raku fired, cone 04
PHOTOS BY PEGGY PETERSON

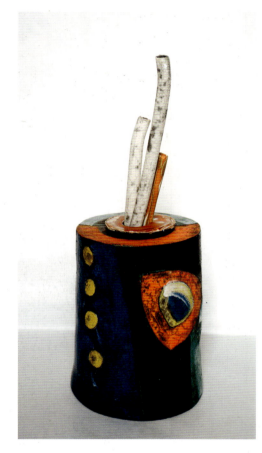

Chiara Nuti
Moods | 2008
50 X 20 INCHES (127 X 50.8 CM)
Hand-built and slab-built raku clay, brushed engobe, underglaze brushwork, gas fired, smoking for reduction
PHOTO BY STEFANIA

Mary Ann Nailos
Awakenings | 2009
8 X 4 X 2½ INCHES (20.3 X 10.2 X 6.4 CM)
Slab-built Balcones White, terra sigillata, paper bag saggar with copper carbonate, salt, sawdust, and steel wool, gas fired, no-reduction air cooling
PHOTO BY ARTIST

Julie Kristin Anderson
Untitled | 2006
4 X 9 X 9 INCHES (10.2 X 22.9 X 22.9 CM)
Wheel-thrown stoneware, sprayed glaze, carved with waxed linen,
macramé and beads, heavy smoking for reduction, cone 05
PHOTO BY TIM MURPHY

Julee Richardson
Warrior | 2009

8 X 8½ X 4 INCHES (20.3 X 21.6 X 10.2 CM)
Press-molded and altered sculpture mix, brushed glaze with latex, carved, overglazed luster, gas-fired raku, smoking through reduction
PHOTO BY DANA DAVIS

Charles Haile
Mythology of Dreams | 2006
10 X 4½ X 4½ INCHES (25.4 X 11.4 X 11.4 CM)
Wheel-thrown Balcones White, chemical dipped and brushed, no glaze,
wire wrapped, gas fired, aluminum foil saggar, no-reduction air cooling
PHOTO BY ARTIST

Carol Russell
Something Lost | 2009
28 X 11 X 11 INCHES (71.1 X 27.9 X 27.9 CM)
Hand-built Laguna Soldate 60, brushed glaze, stains, gas fired, smoking for reduction
PHOTO BY ROSS HILMOE

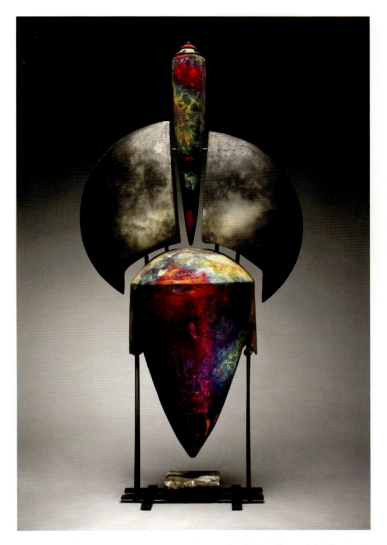

**Heather McQueen
Gregory Milne**
Winged Sentinel Vessel | 2009
75 X 36 X 22 INCHES (190.5 X 91.4 X 55.9 CM)
Press-molded, hand-built, slab-built, and wheel-thrown white raku, sprayed glaze, stamped, electric and gas fired, controlled cooling, smoking for reduction, selective smoking for reduction, cone 018
PHOTO BY ALYCE HENSON

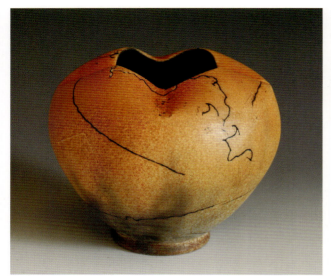

Swanica Ligtenberg
Mashiko Four-Seasons Horsehair Vase | 2006
6 X 6 X 5½ INCHES (15.2 X 15.2 X 14 CM)
Wheel-thrown and altered Orion Stout Stoneware, no glaze, terra sigillata, electric fired, burn on horsehair, smoking with tissue, sprayed with ferric chloride
PHOTO BY ARTIST

Denise Dangora
Spirit Box | 2008
10 X 6 X 6 INCHES (25.4 X 15.2 X 15.2 CM)
Hand-built B-Mix with grog, brushed and sponged glaze, sprigged, stamped, underglaze brushwork, gas fired multiple times, smoking for reduction, cone 06
PHOTO BY ARTIST

Maria Hayden
Teapot with a Twist | 2009
8 X 11 X 3 INCHES (20.3 X 27.9 X 7.6 CM)
Thrown and altered stoneware, brushed glaze with clear crackle, carved, underglazes, gas fired, selective smoking for reduction
PHOTO BY KARA TAYLOR

Stevens Strauss
Tanabata | 2009
4 X 14 X 11 INCHES (10.2 X 35.6 X 27.9 CM)
Slab-built sculpture mix, brushed glaze, gas fired, smoking for reduction
PHOTO BY DANA DAVIS

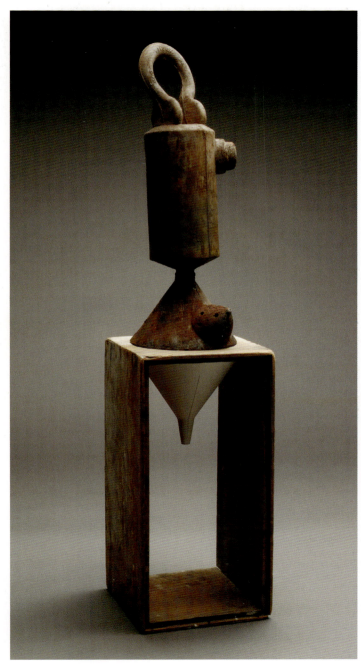

Von Venhuizen
The Phlebotomizer | 2007
40 X 12 X 12 INCHES (101.6 X 30.5 X 30.5 CM)
Slip-cast personal-recipe porcelain, brushed and poured glaze, gas fired, smoking for reduction, cone 04
PHOTO BY ARTIST

Eric L. Stearns
Lifeline | 2009
17 X 13 X 13 INCHES (43.2 X 33 X 33 CM)
Wheel-thrown and pierced personal-recipe clay, brushed glaze, carved, electric fired, selective smoking for reduction
PHOTOS BY ARTIST

Teruhiko (Terry) Hagiwara
Meeting of the Water | 2008

9½ X 8½ INCHES (24.1 X 21.6 CM)

Wheel-thrown personal-recipe clay, painted glaze with brush, gas fired, smoking for reduction

PHOTO BY JACK ZILKER

Irit Lepkin
Temple | 2006

10 X 9 X 5 INCHES (25.4 X 22.9 X 12.7 CM)

Hand-built raku, brushed glaze, carved, gas-fired raku, controlled cooling

PHOTO BY ARTIST

Nina de Creeft Ward
Tribute to an Icon | 2009
27 X 16 X 13 INCHES (68.6 X 40.6 X 33 CM)
Relief-sculpted, hand-built, slab-built, slab-rolled, and formed Laguna Big White, brushed glaze, stamped, sgraffito, gas fired, controlled cooling, smoking for reduction
PHOTO BY ARTIST

Renee Elizabeth Lindquist
Crazy Horsehair | 2009
15 X 8 INCHES (38.1 X 20.3 CM)
Thrown and altered stoneware, no glaze, gas fired, no-reduction
PHOTO BY ARTIST

Ramon Camarillo II
Red Sky at Night | 2009
21 X 14 X 14 INCHES (53.3 X 35.6 X 35.6 CM)
Wheel-thrown Soldate 60, poured glaze, raku fired, fumed, smoking for reduction
PHOTOS BY DONELLE SAWYER CAMARILLO

Lars Westby
Life Preserver Series | 2007
14 X 18 INCHES (35.6 X 45.7 CM)
Press-molded, hand-built, and slab-built Standard 239, brushed glaze, gas fired, smoking for reduction
PHOTO BY ARTIST

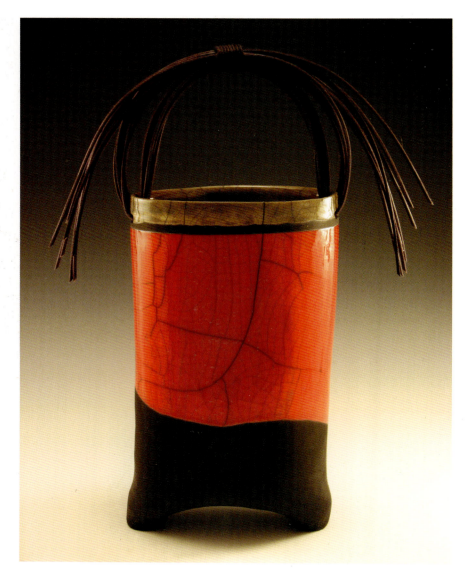

Karen A. Case
Red Crackle Enro | 2007
16 X 10 X 5 INCHES (40.6 X 25.4 X 12.7 CM)
Hand-built Highwater Porcelain, brushed glaze, gas fired, newspaper reduction, cone 06
PHOTO BY ARTIST

Jessica Magaldi
Untitled | 2008

4½ X 5 INCHES (11.4 X 12.7 CM)

Hand-built cone 6-10 personal-recipe stoneware, dipped glaze, carved, propane-fired raku, smoking for reduction

PHOTO BY TODD WEINSTEIN

Loren Maron
Raku Box | 2006

6 X 4½ X 4½ INCHES (15.2 X 11.4 X 11.4 CM)

Thrown and altered Standard Raku, brushed glaze, gas fired, smoking for reduction

PHOTO BY ARTIST

Jana Diedrich
Long Fish | 2008
11 X 24 X 3 INCHES (27.9 X 61 X 7.6 CM)
Hand-built Kyan Raku, sprayed glaze, carved, stamped, gas fired, selective smoking for reduction
PHOTO BY ARTIST

Marlene Angela Kawalez
The Dance | 2009
16½ X 8 X 6 INCHES (41.9 X 20.3 X 15.2 CM)
Hand-built raku, brushed glaze, raku glaze, raku fired, reduced with newspaper and straw
PHOTOS BY ARTIST

Janet Marie Gaddy
Flying Free | 2009
12 X 8 X ¼ INCHES (30.5 X 20.3 X 0.6 CM)
Slab-built, carved, and relief-sculpted Campbell's White Raku, brushed glazes, carved, overglazed, brushed, gas fired, smoking for reduction, quick-fire reduction with newspaper
PHOTO BY TIM MORAN

Steve Aulerich
Untitled | 2008
26 X 8 INCHES (66 X 20.3 CM)
Wheel-thrown Coleman Raku, brushed glaze,
gas fired, smoking for reduction, cone 06
PHOTO BY ARTIST

Holly Sean deSaillan
Five Wall Beetles | 2009
GROUP: 22 X 14 X 1 INCHES (55.9 X 35.6 X 2.5 CM)
Hand-built and slab-built Highwater Clays, brushed glaze with broken glass, stamped, propane fired, selective smoking for reduction
PHOTO BY STEVE MANN

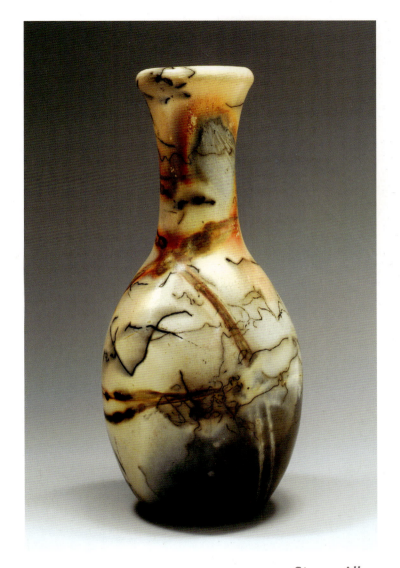

Steven Allen
Cosmic Bottle | 2009
9 X 4 INCHES (22.9 X 10.2 CM)
Wheel-thrown Steve's Stoneware, burnished, gas-fired raku, saggar with sawdust, copper carbonate, salt, copper/salt string, banana peel, post-firing horsehair
PHOTO BY ARTIST

Michel Louis Viala
Untitled | 2007

10 INCHES (25.4 CM) SQUARE

Slab-built Sial Raku, brushed glaze, sgraffito, colored slips, tape resist, gas fired, smoking for reduction, cone 06

PHOTO BY ARTIST

Jim Johnstone
Cortona | 2007

4 X 5½ INCHES (10.2 X 14 CM)

Wheel-thrown porcelain, poured terra sigillata, gas fired, quick smoking

PHOTO BY ARTIST

Miriam Balcazar
Untitled | 2008
10 X 7 INCHES (25.4 X 17.8 CM)
Thrown and carved commercial WSO, brushed glaze, carved, gas fired, smoking for reduction, cone 06
PHOTOS BY ARTIST

Barb Sachs
Storyteller | 2008
11½ X 12 X 4 INCHES (29.2 X 30.5 X 10.2 CM)
Hand-built Tucker's White Sculpture Clay, sprayed glaze, stamped, gas fired, smoking for reduction
PHOTO BY JAMES CHAMBERS

Mary Galligan
Tessellated Fish Series | 2008

5¾ X 15 INCHES (14.6 X 38.1 CM)

Press-molded and altered Standard Ceramic #239 raku, brushed glaze, carved, stamped, gas fired, smoking for reduction in sawdust

PHOTO BY TODD ROTHSTEIN PHOTOGRAPHY

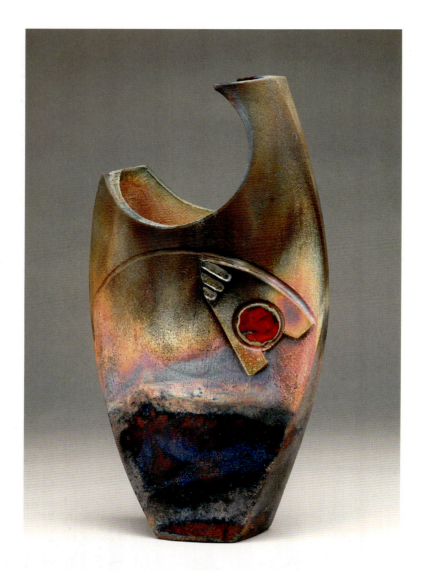

Shaun Hall
Pisces 1 | 2009

14 X 6½ INCHES (35.6 X 16.5 CM)

Slab-built Earthstone Scarva, sprayed copper matte slip, carved, stamped, electric fired, propane fired, reduction, fumed in metal garbage can

PHOTO BY STEPHEN BRAYNE

Maryke Suren Brannin
Untitled | 2005

9 X 5 X 2½ INCHES (22.9 X 12.7 X 6.4 CM)
Hand-built Big White, brushed glazes, underglaze brushwork, gas fired, smoking for reduction, cone 06

PHOTO BY ARTIST

Julia Larkin Price
Wall Flowers | 2009
LARGEST: 18 X 17 X 3 INCHES (45.7 X 43.2 X 7.6 CM)
Hand-built and slab-built 2002, poured glaze, wax-resist brushwork, gas fired, smoking for reduction
PHOTO BY STEVE ZIMMERMAN

Mark S. Weiss
Untitled | 2009

6 X 5½ X 4 INCHES (15.2 X 14 X 10.2 CM)
Relief-sculpted and wheel-thrown raku clay, brushed glaze, carved, gas fired, quick cooling in water, smoking for reduction
PHOTO BY SAL CORDARO

Deborah G. Rodgers
Untitled | 2009

7 X 18 INCHES (17.8 X 45.7 CM)
Wheel-thrown and altered white stone, brushed glaze, carved, stamped, gas-fired raku, smoking for reduction
PHOTO BY DAN RODGERS

Linda Willard
Naked Eggs | 2007

5 X 10 X 9 INCHES (12.7 X 25.4 X 22.9 CM)
Hand-built and slab-built Laguna WSO, naked raku, poured slip and glaze, propane-fired raku, smoking

PHOTO BY ARTIST

Timothy Winspear Moran
Sunrise | 2008
26 X 22 X 5 INCHES (66 X 55.9 X 12.7 CM)
Wheel-thrown, altered, stamped, and sprigged Standard 119, sprayed glaze and luster, quick reduction in paper, post-reduction torching for flashing
PHOTO BY ARTIST

Phyllis Pacin
Shoestring Tree | 2008
16 X 21 INCHES (40.6 X 53.3 CM)
Hand-rolled and textured personal-recipe clay, brushed and sponged glaze, wax resist, gas fired, smoking for reduction
PHOTO BY SIBILA SAVAGE

Cathleen Scanlan
Loon | 2009

7½ X 16½ X 7 INCHES (19.1 X 41.9 X 17.8 CM)
Hand-built low-fire raku, brushed glaze, underglaze brushwork, mason stains, gas fired, smoking for reduction

PHOTO BY KARL DENNIS

Marvin Sweet
Bisnaga 9 | 2009
16 X 13 X 13 INCHES (40.6 X 33 X 33 CM)
Hand-built and slab-built personal-recipe clay, sprayed glaze, paint, non-fired, gas fired, smoking for reduction
PHOTO BY LISA NUGENT

Joan Carcia
Naked Raku—Blue Field | 2009

4 X 4½ X 4½ INCHES (10.2 X 11.4 X 11.4 CM)
Hand-built Sheffield S14 clay, dipped slip and glaze, terra sigillata, gas fired, smoking for reduction
PHOTO BY ARTIST

Eileen McDaniel
Untitled | 2008

7 X 7 X 7 INCHES (17.8 X 17.8 X 17.8 CM)
Wheel-thrown Soldate, brushed glaze, electric fired, controlled cooling, smoking for reduction
PHOTO BY DALE ANDERSON

Nicki Berndt
Orange and Blue Raku Jug | 2009
10½ x 7 INCHES (26.7 X 17.8 CM)
Wheel-thrown and extruded Balcones, dipped glaze, gas fired, smoking for reduction
PHOTO BY ARTIST

Erin Ryan
Desolation | 2007

15 x 6 x 6 INCHES (38.1 x 15.2 x 15.2 CM)
Slab-built B-Mix with sand, unglazed, colored stains, gas fired, smoking for reduction

PHOTO BY LARRY LYTLE

Ronnie Gould
Rooster | 2007
10 X 5 X 11 INCHES (25.4 X 12.7 X 27.9 CM)
Hand-built Sheffield S-14, brushed glaze, gas fired, smoking for reduction
PHOTO BY ARTIST

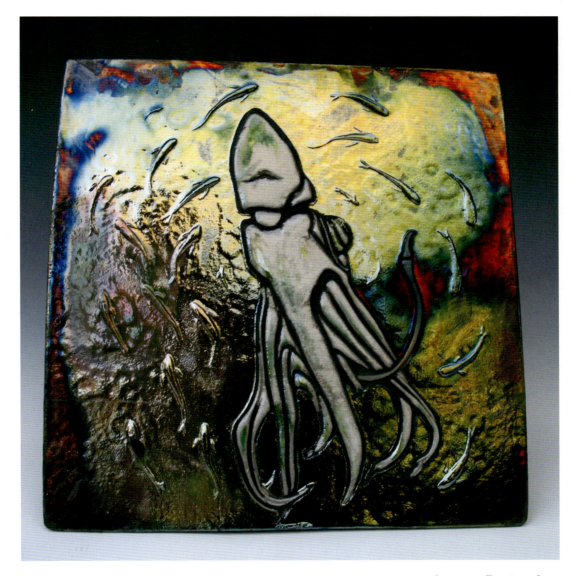

Jeremy Barton Lea
Cryptic Coloration | 2009
10½ X 10 X ¼ INCHES (26.7 X 25.4 X 0.6 CM)
Slab-built and relief-sculpted Campbell's White Raku, brushed glaze, carved, gas fired, smoking for reduction, cone 06
PHOTO BY TIM MORAN

Rosemary Aiello
Lone Star | 2008
9 X 13 X 13 INCHES (22.9 X 33 X 33 CM)
Press-molded, coiled, and thrown Ceramic Supply #295, naked raku, gas-fired raku, smoking for reduction, heavy reduction, cooling in water
PHOTO BY GEORGE POTANIVIC

Jessica Broad
This One's for Ellie | 2009

13 x 20 x 14 INCHES (33 X 50.8 X 35.6 CM)

Press-molded, hand-built, and coiled white stoneware, brushed glaze, underglaze brushwork, gas fired, smoking for reduction

PHOTO BY ARTIST

Mona Michelle Shiber
Ha•tha: Union of Opposites | 2006
36 X 36 X 3½ INCHES (91.4 X 91.4 X 8.9 CM)
Relief sculpted, hand-built, slab-built, and coiled groggy stoneware and porcelain slip, carved, bisque fired, gas fired, selective smoking for reduction, cones 3, 03, and 06
PHOTO BY JOHN POLAK

Joan Pevarnik
Slice of Life | 2009

5 X 2 X 4 INCHES (12.7 X 5.1 X 10.2 CM)

Hand-built Big White with slabs, poured glaze, stamped, propane fired, reduction with paper

PHOTO BY MARTHA LOCHERT

Marcia Reiver
Dragonfly Mission | 2009

28 X 8 INCHES (71.1 X 20.3 CM)

Wheel-thrown Standard 239, brushed glaze, taped design, gas fired, controlled cooling, smoking and cooling in water

PHOTO BY JOHN CARLANO

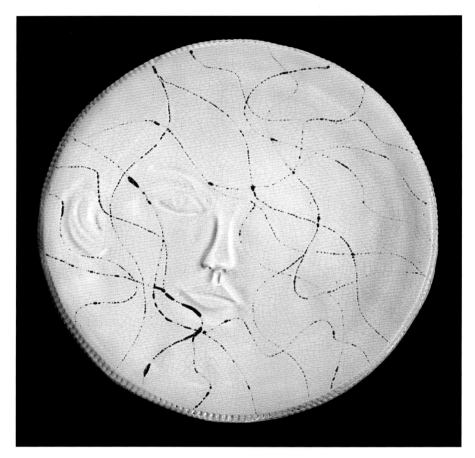

Betty L. Wilson
Slipping through the Cracks | 2009
19 INCHES (48.2 CM) IN DIAMETER
Relief sculpted, hand-built, and slab-built Cheryl-Tall Red, brushed glaze, crackle overglazed, carved, oxide wash, electric fired, quick smoking, cone 6
PHOTO BY DURGA GARCIA

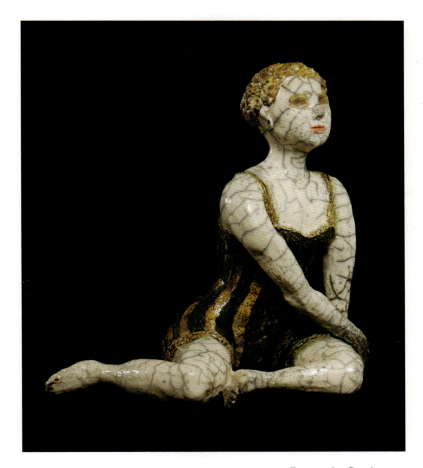

Dora A. Savignac
Ms. Kyner | 2009
6 X 6 X 4 INCHES (15.2 X 15.2 X 10.2 CM)
Hand-built wood fire clay 470, brushed glaze, carved, underglaze brushwork, oxide wash, propane fired, smoking for reduction, 1900°F (1038°C)
PHOTO BY NICK SHAWMAN

David Scott Smith
Louisiana Gothic (with Bullfrog) | 2009
21 X 14 X 3 INCHES (53.3 X 35.6 X 7.6 CM)
Press-molded, relief-sculpted, hand-built, slab-built, and extruded personal-recipe clay, brushed glaze, carved, sprigged, stamped, gas fired, smoking for reduction, cone 08
PHOTO BY ARTIST

John Patrick Mitchell
Maneater | 2007
14 X 9½ X 9 INCHES (35.6 X 24.1 X 22.9 CM)
Hand-built Sheffield S14, dipped glaze,
gas fired, smoking for reduction
PHOTO BY ARTIST

Ilona Sauša
Cougars in the Walk | 2007

7 X 19 X 5½ INCHES (18 X 48 X 14 CM)

Press-molded and hand-built white chammote, sgraffito, oxide wash, gas fired, smoking for reduction, quick cooling, cone 05

PHOTO BY JANIS MAGDALENOKS

Laura L. Demme
Nest | 2008
18 X 10 X 5 INCHES (45.7 X 25.4 X 12.7 CM)
Press-molded, hand-built, and carved Standard 239 Raku, brushed and sponged glaze, carved, gas fired, smoking for reduction
PHOTO BY BARB TERENZI CHALMERS

John S. Chianelli
Solar Flair | 2007

11 X 12½ X 5½ INCHES (27.9 X 31.8 X 14 CM)

Hand-built, wheel-thrown, and extruded commercial raku, brushed glaze, brushed and burnished terra sigillata, mixed-media embellishments, natural gas fired, heavy smoking, slow cooling in post-firing chamber for finish, cone 08

PHOTO BY PETER LEE

Nina Kellogg
Red, Yellow, Orange in Black and White | 2005

60 X 72 INCHES (152.4 X 182.9 CM)

Slab-built WSO Stoneware, brushed glaze, masking tape, gas fired, smoking for reduction, cone 06

PHOTO BY ANTHONY CUNHA

Jeffrey A. Schwarz
Untitled | 2009

12 X 10 X 10 INCHES (30.5 X 25.4 X 25.4 CM)

Press-molded and hand-built personal-recipe clay, terra sigillata, naked raku, gas fired, smoking for reduction

PHOTO BY ARTIST

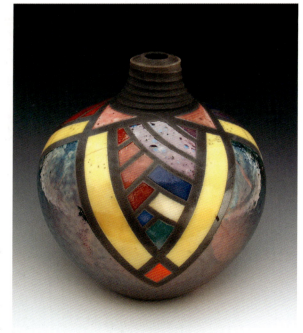

Teri Lee
Vase | 2007

16½ X 7 INCHES (41.9 X 17.8 CM)

Wheel-thrown Rod's Bod, brushed glaze, taped, gas fired, smoking for reduction

PHOTO BY ARTIST

Shirley Al
Dancer | 2007
15 X 11¾ X 5½ INCHES (38.1 X 29.8 X 14 CM)
Hand-built raku, brushed glaze,
gas fired, smoking for reduction
PHOTO BY SHERI VISAKALY

Joan Tanzer
Woman in Batik Robe | 2007
18 X 17 X 3½ INCHES (45.7 X 43.2 X 8.9 CM)
Hand-built and slab-built sculpture mix, brushed glaze, stamped, embellished with silver and amethysts, gas fired, smoking for reduction
PHOTO BY ARTIST

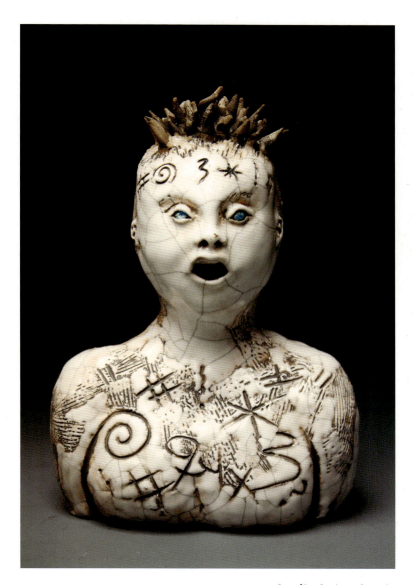

Leslie Laine Lewis
@#%! | 2007

8½ X 6½ X 3½ INCHES (21.6 X 16.5 X 8.9 CM)
Hand-built and coiled earthenware, carved,
electric fired, quick smoking, cone 04

PHOTO BY ARTIST

Andrew Patrick Linton
Inquisitive Spiral Horse | 2008
18 x 16 x 7 INCHES (45.7 x 40.6 x 17.8 CM)
Hand-built, slab-built, hump-molded, and extruded Phoenix-Highwater, brushed glaze, carved, stamped, incised, gas fired, cone 04, smoking for reduction in sawdust and shredded paper
PHOTO BY SHANE BASKIN

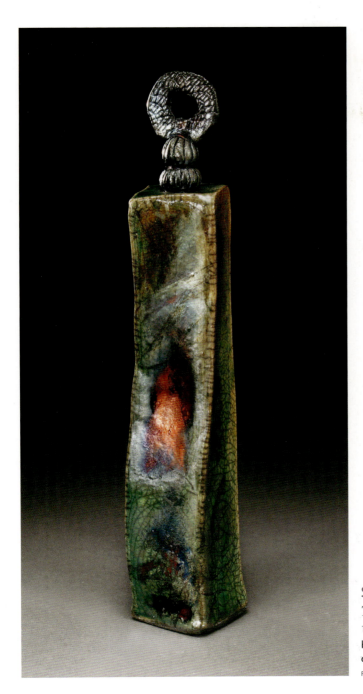

Shane Baskin
Twisted Box-Bottle with Copper Accent | 2005
12 X 2½ X 2½ INCHES (30.5 X 6.4 X 6.4 CM)
Hand-built and slab-built Highwater Raku,
dipped glaze, carved, stamped, gas fired, cone 04
PHOTO BY ARTIST

Dinah Sheeran Stonis
Canticle V | 2009
20 X 7 INCHES (50.8 X 17.8 CM)
Hand-built and wheel-thrown Kickwheel Pottery Raku, brushed and dipped glaze, raku fired, controlled cooling, smoking for reduction
PHOTO BY WALKER MONTGOMERY

Avis Akers Cherichetti
Flower Stone | 2009
3½ X 4½ INCHES (8.9 X 11.4 CM)
Thrown and altered Laguna 510, sprayed glaze, gas fired, selective smoking for reduction, heavy reduction with pine needles and cones
PHOTO BY ARTIST

John A. Reinking III
Fossilized Mulberry Bottle | 2009
12 X 5 INCHES (30.5 X 12.7 CM)
Wheel-thrown personal-recipe clay, unglazed, gas fired, quick smoking with fresh foliage
PHOTO BY ARTIST

Daryl Shafran
Untitled | 2009
9 X 10 X 10 INCHES (22.9 X 25.4 X 25.4 CM)
Wheel-thrown stoneware, brushed glaze, textured, gas fired, smoking for reduction
PHOTO BY ARTIST

Carol Rossman
Barcelona Series #4 | 2007
5½ x 8½ x 8½ INCHES (14 X 21.6 X 21.6 CM)
Wheel-thrown Michael Sheba Raku, brushed and sprayed glazes, burnished terra sigillata, glazes, oxides, propane fired, reduction in sawdust and newspaper, quick re-oxidation, cone 08
PHOTO BY MICHAEL DISMATSEK

Jon Budas
Nebula | 2009

14 X 5/8 INCHES (35.6 X 1.6 CM)
Wheel-thrown Sculpture Raku, poured glaze,
gas-fired raku, smoking for reduction, cone 07
PHOTO BY DEBORAH E. BALLIN

Helen Johnson
Untitled | 2006

7½ X 4½ X 14⅛ INCHES (19.1 X 11.4 X 35.9 CM)

Wheel-thrown 181 white stoneware, brushed glaze, India ink, gas fired, air cooled, smoked

PHOTO BY EDDIE ING

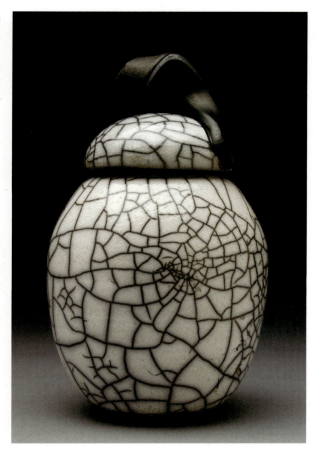

Catherine J. Rehbein
Floralnimity | 2008

14 X 4 X 2½ INCHES (35.6 X 10.2 X 6.4 CM)

Extruded and altered Rovins Raku, sprayed and dipped glaze, copper leaf additions, gas fired, smoked chamber reduction

PHOTO BY ARTIST

Linda Epstein
Untitled | 2009
8 X 10¼ INCHES (20.3 X 26 CM)
Wheel-thrown Laguna Soldate, brushed glaze, carved, gas fired, smoking for reduction
PHOTO BY ARTIST

Lynda Farmer
Medium Billowy Pot | 2009
4 X 9½ X 3½ INCHES (10.2 X 24.1 X 8.9 CM)
Hand-built Umpqua, brushed glaze, distended, gas-fired raku, newspaper in trashcan, cone 06
PHOTO BY LINDA STEPHENS

Justin R. Manfredi
Acid Healer | 2008
8 X 10½ X 6½ INCHES (20.3 X 26.7 X 16.5 CM)
Hand-built stoneware, brushed glaze, gas fired, smoking for reduction
PHOTO BY ARTIST

Wally Asselberghs
Pisces | 2009
5¾ X 8 X 2¾ INCHES (14.6 X 20.3 X 7 CM)
Coiled Westerwald Fine Grog Stoneware, naked raku sacrificial slip and glaze, splashed glaze, propane fired, selective smoking for reduction
PHOTO BY JOE MEHL

Dawn Angela Dyer
Suspended Secrets | 2008
22 X 8 X 31 INCHES (55.9 X 20.3 X 78.7 CM)
Wood-fired slip-cast clay with bronze attachment, naked raku glaze, raku fired, smoking for reduction
PHOTO BY ARTIST

John Ignarri
Ritual Vessel | 2005

7½ X 5¼ X 19½ INCHES (19.1 X 13.3 X 49.5 CM)

Wheel-thrown Standard Raku #238, poured glaze, thermal-shock crazing, gas fired, controlled cooling, quick smoking

PHOTO BY ARTIST

Michael James Chambers
Vase Green | 2009

12 X 6 X 2½ INCHES (30.5 X 15.2 X 6.4 CM)

Hand-built and slab-built stoneware, brushed glaze, stamped, thick slip, gas fired, smoking for reduction

PHOTO BY ARTIST

Vicki Rapport Paulet
Bathers | 2007
7 X 10 INCHES (17.8 X 25.4 CM)
Wheel-thrown and sculpted white stoneware, gas fired, smoking for reduction, no-reduction air cooling
PHOTO BY EDDIE ING

Kara Taylor
Pillow Talk | 2005
12 X 14 X 6 INCHES (30.5 X 35.6 X 15.2 CM)
Hand-built and slab-constructed stoneware, brushed glaze, carved, wax resist, gas fired, controlled cooling, lid burping for smoking reduction
PHOTO BY ARTIST

Dorothy Louise Deschamps
Seed Rock | 2009
10 x 11 x 8 INCHES (25.4 x 27.9 x 20.3 CM)
Hand-built paper clay, brushed glaze, raku fired, raku reduction
PHOTO BY RENÉ FUNK

Scott Kristian Stockdale
Untitled | 2009
12 X 8 INCHES (30.5 X 20.3 CM)
Wheel-thrown, thrown, and altered Highwater Clay Moon White Stoneware, brushed glaze, stained glass applied during firing, gas fired, quick cooling in water, reduction in newspaper
PHOTO BY ARTIST

David T. Collins
Untitled | 2009
11 X 11 X 16 INCHES (27.9 X 27.9 X 40.6 CM)
Slip cast personal-recipe clay, brushed glaze, naked raku, gas fired, smoking for reduction, cone 08
PHOTO BY ARTIST

Reg Brown
Oldest Warrior | 2006
14 X 15 X 15 INCHES (35.6 X 38.1 X 38.1 CM)
Wheel-thrown Miller/Laguna Soldate 60, naked raku, gas fired, smoking for reduction
PHOTO BY GREGORY R. STALEY

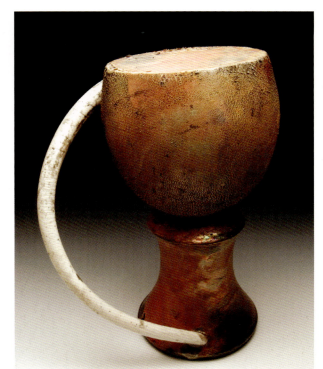

Matthew Bright
The Simple Things | 2009
15 X 8 X 8 INCHES (38.1 X 20.3 X 20.3 CM)
Hand-built, slab-built, wheel-thrown, and pulled personal-recipe clay, sprayed and dipped glaze, gas fired, controlled cooling, smoking for reduction
PHOTO BY ARTIST

Genez Gilley Malebranche
Sticking His Neck Out | 2008
9½ X 7¼ INCHES (24.1 X 18.4 CM)
Wheel-thrown, turned, and carved Highwater Helios Porcelain, splashed glaze, electric fired, reduction in a pit fire
PHOTO BY ARTIST

Ana England
Shared Identity: Wave and Galaxy with Thumbprints | 2006

23½ X 23½ INCHES (59.7 X 59.7 CM)

Press-molded Standard Clay Low-Fire White, burnished, unglazed, carved, gas-fired raku, post-fire selective smoking in sawdust, cone 09

PHOTOS BY ARTIST

Mia Lindberg
She's Come Undone | 2009
22 X 13 X 10 INCHES (55.9 X 33 X 25.4 CM)
Hand-built Axner, brushed and sponged glaze, carved, faceted, stamped, gas-fired raku, controlled cooling, smoking for reduction
PHOTO BY MICHAEL A. SCHILLACI

Vickie Edwards
Freedom | 2005
9½ X 7 X 7 INCHES (24.1 X 17.8 X 17.8 CM)
Thrown and altered Standard Raku, brushed glaze, gas fired, smoking for reduction
PHOTO BY EDDIE ING

Jao-O Beatrice Chang
YinYang Series #5: Ru Yi | 2005
TALLEST: 18 X 20 X 6½ INCHES (45.7 X 50.8 X 16.5 CM)

Thrown and altered Ceramic Supply #239 Raku, brushed glaze, Chinese calligraphy, outlined, gas fired, selective smoking for reduction
PHOTO BY ARTIST

Ruth Ann Reese
Oracle | 2009
18 X 12 X 3 INCHES (45.7 X 30.5 X 7.6 CM)
Hand-built, slab-built, and sculpted raku and earthenware, painted glaze, iron oxide wash, assembled, grouted, electric fired, raku, smoking for reduction in a trash can
PHOTO BY ARTIST

Beverly Helaine Fetterman
Gourd-Shaped Vessel | 2009

13 X 8½ X 8½ INCHES (33 X 21.6 X 21.6 CM)

Wheel-thrown Balcones White Stoneware, tape resist, salt-soaked materials, wax resist, stains with iron chloride, raku fired with tin foil wrapping, selective smoking for reduction

PHOTO BY CHRIS GRAY

Suzanne Stumpf
Matchbox | 2005

5 X 3⅛ X 3⅛ INCHES (12.7 X 7.9 X 7.9 CM)

Hand-built, thrown, and altered Miller Porcelain, dipped glaze, gas fired, smoking for reduction

PHOTO BY JOHN POLAK

Gail Rushmore
For the Yellow River | 2006
25 X 6 X 6 INCHES (63.5 X 15.2 X 15.2 CM)
Hand-built and slab-built Laguna WSO, unglazed, underglaze brushwork, gas fired, smoking for reduction
PHOTO BY HAP SAKWA

Theresa A. Glisson
Untitled | 2009
7 X 5 X 2¼ INCHES (17.8 X 12.7 X 5.7 CM)
Press-molded cone-10 stoneware, sprayed glaze, gas fired, smoking for reduction
PHOTO BY ARTIST

Martin Stankus
Untitled | 2009
9 X 6½ X 6½ INCHES (22.9 X 16.5 X 16.5 CM)
Wheel-thrown Highwater Clays Raku, brushed glaze,
taped resist, gas fired, smoking for reduction
PHOTO BY LYNN RUCK

Jack W. Valentine
Water Meter T-Pot | 2009
16 X 11 X 5 INCHES (40.6 X 27.9 X 12.7 CM)
Press-molded and slab-built personal-recipe clay, brushed glaze, overglazed, gas fired, smoking for reduction
PHOTO BY ANTONIO DAVIS

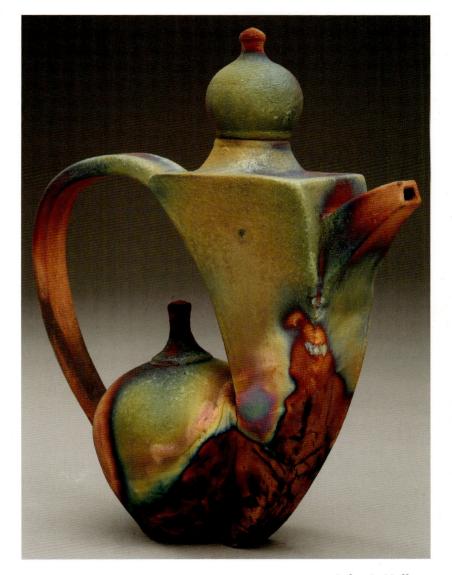

John J. Kellum
Deco Teapot | 2008
14 x 12 x 6 INCHES (35.6 x 30.5 x 15.2 CM)
Slab-built and wheel-thrown Elena's Raku/Axner, sprayed glaze, gas fired, smoking for reduction with burping
PHOTO BY RANDALL SMITH

Marilyn Proctor-Givens
Spherical Puzzle | 2005
13 INCHES (33 CM) TALL
Slab-built raku clay, brushed glaze, carved, gas fired, smoking for reduction, sprayed with water, salt fired
PHOTO BY ARTIST

Phyllis Elizabeth Canupp
Fear | 2009
4 X 10 X 14 INCHES (10.2 X 25.4 X 35.6 CM)
Hand-built and slab-built Campbell's Raku, brushed glaze, gas fired, smoking for reduction, cone 06
PHOTO BY ARTIST

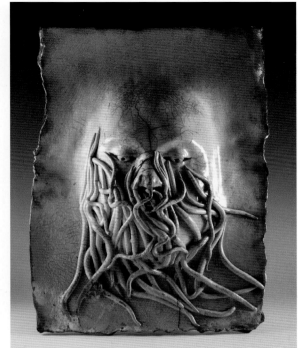

Steve Loucks
Lobed Form #2 | 2008
15½ X 8 X 8½ INCHES (39.4 X 20.3 X 21.6 CM)
Soft-slab and hand-built Raku #238, brushed glaze, textured, gas fired, smoke reduction in sawdust
PHOTO BY ARTIST

Jim Manna
Aurora Mist | 2009
8½ X 8 INCHES (21.6 X 20.3 CM)
Stretch-thrown smooth raku, sprayed glaze, propane fired, controlled cooling
PHOTO BY ARTIST

Shelby Banks Duensing
Boxed In | 2005

SQUARE BOX: 5 X 3½ X 2½ INCHES (12.7 X 8.8 X 6.3 CM)
ROUND BOX: 5 X 4½ X 4½ INCHES (12.7 X 11.4 X 11.4 CM)

Thrown and altered Highwater Loafer's Glory clay, brushed glaze, sticker and tape resist, non-ceramic beads, wire, gas fired, smoking for reduction

PHOTO BY JASON STEELMAN

Lynnette Hesser
Spiral Wall Piece | 2006

40 INCHES (101.6 CM) SQUARE

Rolled-out slab #238 Raku, brushed glaze, carved, textured, gas fired, slow smoking in sawdust

PHOTO BY STEVE LOUCKS

Joellen Varsalona Schillaci
Gliding | 2008
3 X 8 X 9 INCHES (7.6 X 20.3 X 22.9 CM)
Hand-built Axner, brushed glaze, carved, gas fired raku,
selective smoking for reduction, controlled cooling
PHOTO BY MICHAEL A. SCHILLACI

Lin M. Holley
Maria's Retablo | 2007

13 X 10 X 4 INCHES (33 X 25.4 X 10.2 CM)

Hand-built and slab-built Coleman Raku, assembled, brushed glaze, carved, stamped, gas-fired raku, electric low-fired, smoking for reduction, cone 05

PHOTO BY ROGER SCHREIBER

Dina Angel-Wing
Better Half Teapot | 2006
18 X 12 X 8 INCHES (45.7 X 30.5 X 20.3 CM)
Wheel-thrown and altered stoneware, brushed and dipped glaze, overglazed, gas-fired raku, quick smoking
PHOTO BY FRANK WING

Glenn Trotter
Untitled | 2009
7 X 4¾ X 5½ INCHES (17.8 X 12.1 X 14 CM)
Wheel-thrown and assembled Laguna Raku K White,
brushed and sprayed glaze, gas fired, smoking for reduction
PHOTO BY LEIGH COSBY

Leigh Cosby
Offering | 2009

21 X 9½ X 7½ INCHES (53.3 X 24.1 X 19.1 CM)

Thrown, pierced, and hand-built Laguna Raku K, sprayed and brushed glaze, stamped, sprigged, pine needles, African Jasper, onyx beads, wire, gas fired, smoking for reduction

PHOTO BY ARTIST

Paul F. Morris
Untitled Lidded Stack Pot | 2009

31½ X 10 X 10 INCHES (80 X 25.4 X 25.4 CM)

Wheel-thrown personal-recipe clay, brushed glaze, gas fired, smoking for reduction

PHOTO BY ARTIST

Diane Gilbert
Baby Egrets | 2009
10 X 8 X 7 INCHES (25.4 X 20.3 X 17.8 CM)
Slab-built raku clay, brushed glaze, carved, underglaze, gas fired, smoking for reduction, cone 06
PHOTO BY ARTIST

Tammy Tomczyk-Jackson
Garden Ants | 2009
LARGEST: 8¼ X 5 X 7 INCHES (20.9 X 12.7 X 17.8 CM)
Slab-built, formed, and pierced cone 04 white raku, formed steel rod
and wire addition, brushed glaze, electric fired, smoking for reduction
PHOTO BY ARTIST

Joyce Hayter
Altered Plate | 2009

10 X 10 X 1 INCHES (25.4 X 25.4 X 2.5 CM)

Hand and slab-built Standard 239 Raku, brushed, sponged, and dripped glaze, carved, stamped, gas fired, smoking for reduction

PHOTO BY ARTIST

Dale Sell
Candle Bowl | 2009

6 X 7 X 7 INCHES (15.2 X 17.8 X 17.8 CM)

Hand-built B-Mix, brushed glaze, carved, gas fired, smoking for reduction

PHOTO BY JOHN OLIVER LEWIS

Cindy Hoskisson
Untitled | 2009
7½ X 8 INCHES (19.1 X 20.3 CM)
Wheel-thrown Laguna B-Mix, brushed and dipped glaze,
stamped, gas fired, smoking for reduction, cone 06
PHOTO BY DON HOSKISSON

Gary L. Ratcliff
Untitled | 2009
6 X 12 INCHES (15.2 X 30.5 CM)
Wheel-thrown personal-recipe clay, burnished, terra sigillata, horsehair, iron chloride, gas fired, selective smoking for reduction
PHOTO BY JOLI LAVAUDAIS GRISHAM

Cynthia J. Williams
Cherokee Angel | 2007
20 X 10 X 3 INCHES (50.8 X 25.4 X 7.6 CM)
Hand-built personal high-fire clay, brushed glaze, carved, stamped, gold leaf, gas fired, smoking for reduction
PHOTO BY ARTIST

Lindsey Epstein
Untitled | 2007
13½ x 10½ x 6 INCHES (34.3 X 26.7 X 15.2 CM)
Hand-built personal-recipe clay, brushed glaze, gas fired, smoking for reduction
PHOTO BY ARTIST

Kristen Giles
Dragon Whistle | 2009
7 X 3½ INCHES (17.7 X 8.8 CM)
Hand-built Balcones Armadillo, brushed glaze, carved, stamped, gas fired, smoking for reduction
PHOTO BY HARRISON EVANS

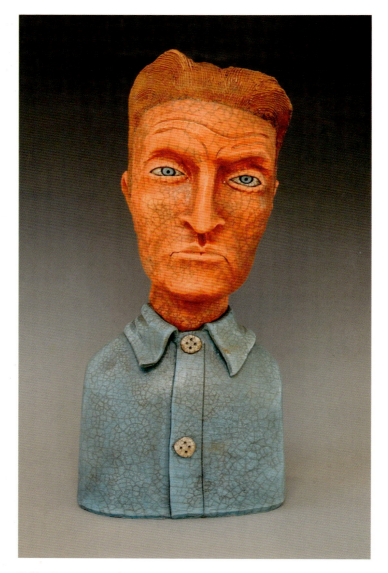

Billy Ray Mangham
Berger Engblon—Petty Theft | 2009
29 X 8 X 8 INCHES (73.7 X 20.3 X 20.3 CM)
Thrown and slab-built Armadillo Clay and Raku, brushed glaze, gas fired, compressed air reduction with newspaper
PHOTO BY TY JOHNSON

Steven Edward Hemingway
Summer (Cygnus) | 2009

36 X 24 X 2 INCHES (91.4 X 61 X 5.1 CM)
Slab-built and wheel-thrown Continental Clay Smooth Stoneware, brushed glaze, carved, sprigged, gas fired, controlled cooling, smoking for reduction in sawdust, cone 06

PHOTO BY ARTIST

Marcia L. Selsor
Grazers | 2006
22 X 20½ X 1 INCHES (55.9 X 52.1 X 2.5 CM)
Slab-built Piepenburg Raku with paper pulp, sprayed glaze, luster lime, propane-fired raku, smoking with newspaper in can, cone 06
PHOTO BY ARTIST

David Schembri
Tectonic Shift | 2008
48 X 36 X 3 INCHES (121.9 X 91.4 X 7.6 CM)
Slab-built Sheba Raku Clay, brushed and sponged glaze,
impressed, stamped, layered, gas fired, smoking for reduction
PHOTO BY CLEO TOBIAS

Steven Sanchez
Moon Myth | 2009
9½ X 7 INCHES (24.1 X 17.8 CM)
Wheel-thrown cone 10 white stoneware, brushed glaze,
gas-fired raku, pre-air cooling, smoking for reduction
PHOTOS BY LOREN NELSON

Bob Clyatt
Re-Emergence of the Path | 2009
12 x 8 x 7 INCHES (30.5 x 20.3 x 17.8 CM)
Hand-built Tucker's Sandstone, brushed glaze,
gas fired, smoking for reduction, cone 05
PHOTO BY ARTIST

Anthony J. Foo
Japanese Demon Masks | 2008
EACH: 10 X 7½ X 4½ INCHES (25.4 X 19.1 X 11.4 CM)
Press-molded and hand-built Imco Paper Clay, brushed glaze, gas fired, smoking for reduction, raku, cone 06
PHOTO BY ARTIST

Richard N. Jackson
Say #13 | 2007
18 X 15 X 6 INCHES (45.7 X 38.1 X 15.2 CM)
Hand-built stoneware, brushed glaze, overglazed, gas fired, quick smoking
PHOTO BY ARTIST

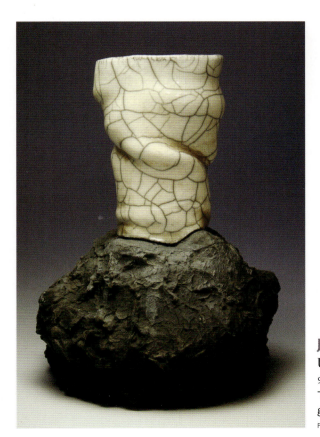

Juan Manuel Zavala
Untitled | 2009
9 X 7 X 7 INCHES (22.9 X 17.8 X 17.8 CM)
Thrown and altered stoneware, brushed glaze, gas fired, smoking for reduction
PHOTO BY JOHN OLIVER LEWIS

Linda Hansen Mau
Brocade Kimono | 2008
15 x 12½ x 5 INCHES (38.1 X 31.8 X 12.7 CM)
Slab-built B-Mix with grog, brushed glaze, gas fired, strong reduction
PHOTO BY ARTIST

John Evans
Talking Heads | 2007
15 INCHES (38.1 CM) TALL
Hand-built Scarva PF520, terra sigillata, resist slip and glaze, gas fired, naked raku, quick smoking, cone 08 bisque
PHOTO BY ARTIST

Nadeige Choplet
L'Insolente (The Insolent) | 2009
22½ X 16 X 3¼ INCHES (57.2 X 40.6 X 8.3 CM)
Hand-built and slab-built Laguna Porcelain, brushed glaze, gas fired, smoking for reduction, cone 04
PHOTO BY ARTIST

Ann Currie
Untitled | 2009
5 X 2 X 4 INCHES (12.7 X 5.1 X 10.2 CM)
Thrown and altered personal-recipe clay, brushed glaze, stamped, gas fired, quick smoking
PHOTO BY WAYNE HORTON

Wayne Horton
Spirit Platter | 2008
2 X 8 X 8 INCHES (5.1 X 20.3 X 20.3 CM)
Slab-built personal-recipe clay, brushed glaze, wax resist, gas fired, smoking for reduction
PHOTO BY ARTIST

Shari Sikora
Untitled | 2006

4 X 3 X 3 INCHES (10.2 X 7.6 X 7.6 CM)
Hand-built Standard Raku 239, brushed glaze, propane fired, air cooling
PHOTO BY CAROL ROPER

Zac Hould
Lidded Globe | 2009
10 X 8 X 9 INCHES (25.4 X 20.3 X 22.9 CM)
Wheel-thrown Aardvark Soldate 60, brushed glaze, gas fired, smoking for reduction, cone 06
PHOTO BY PETER ZAKHARY

Frederick de la Cruz
Untitled | 2009
3 X 20 X 6 INCHES (7.6 X 50.8 X 15.2 CM)
Slab-built Rod's Bod, brushed glaze, gas fired, smoking for reduction
PHOTO BY ARTIST

Evamarie Pappas
Untitled | 2007

26 X 7 INCHES (66 X 17.8 CM)
Wheel-thrown Raku 250, wax resist,
brushed glaze, gas fired, quick smoking
PHOTO BY ERIC OGLANDER

Reid Takahashi
Twisted Vase | 2008

11 X 3½ X 3½ INCHES (27.9 X 8.9 X 8.9 CM)
Extruded and altered Laguna WC-389, brushed glaze,
carved, faceted, gas fired, smoking for reduction
PHOTO BY ARTIST

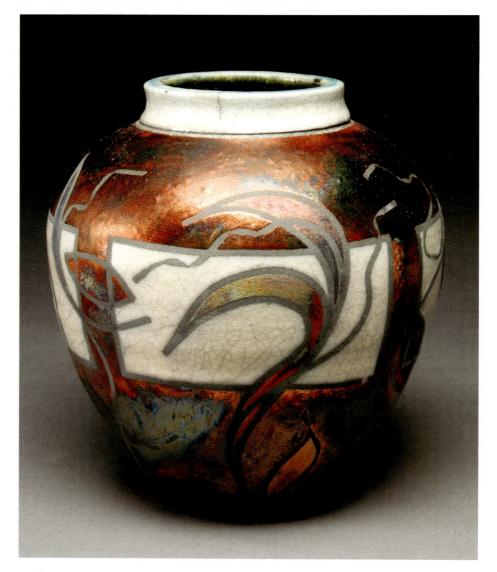

Debra Katz Sampson
Copper Leaves in Window Raku Vase | 2009
10 x 7 INCHES (25.4 x 17.8 CM)
Wheel-thrown raku clay, brushed glaze with resist, multi-glazed, electric fired, reduction in bucket with newspaper
PHOTO BY GUY NICOL

Douglas E. Gray
Urn: Begotten | 2008
10 X 9 X 4 INCHES (25.4 X 22.9 X 10.2 CM)
Hand-built personal-recipe clay, brushed glaze, black wax resist, stamped, ink transfer, gas fired, smoking for reduction
PHOTO BY ARTIST

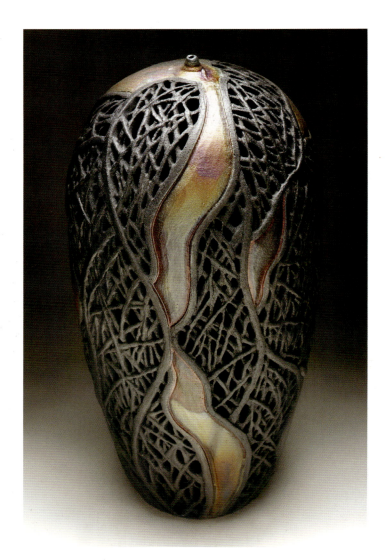

Diane KW
Joel Park
Lava Flowing | 2009
16 INCHES (40.6 CM) TALL
Wheel-thrown Soldate 60, sponged glaze, hand carved and pierced, gas fired, smoking for reduction
PHOTO BY CORY LUM

Ken Malson
Mama, Where You Keep Your Pistol | 2009
15 X 11 X 7 INCHES (38.1 X 27.9 X 17.8 CM)
Slip-cast cone 10 stoneware slip, brushed glaze, gas-fired raku, reduction air cooling
PHOTO BY WESLEY HARVEY

Carol Smeraldo

Under-Sea Fleet: Rock the Boat—The Energy and Inspiration of Chaos, in Four Parts: Mother Boat, Carrier Boat, Learned Boat, and Closed Boat | 2009

DIMENSIONS VARIABLE

Hand-built, slab-built, and wheel-thrown local earthenware and Tucker's Raku, naked-raku slip resist, terra sigillata, gas fired, smoking for reduction

PHOTO BY ARTIST

Simcha Even-Chen
Illusion III | 2009
7⅞ X 24 X 26 INCHES (20 X 61 X 66 CM)
Slab-built Vingerling K129, naked raku, masking technique, gas fired, quick smoking
PHOTO BY ILAN AMIHAI

Jennifer Brazelton
Baby's Breath | 2009
6 X 6 X 3 INCHES (15.2 X 15.2 X 7.6 CM)
Press-molded, extruded, thrown, and hand-built
Sculpture Mix 412, brushed glaze, sprigged, underglazed,
gas fired, smoking for reduction
PHOTO BY WILFRED J. JONES

Vineeta D. Agarwal
Escapement | 2008
10 X 6 X 4 INCHES (25.4 X 15.2 X 10.2 CM)
Thrown and altered B-Mix, brushed glaze, carved,
gas fired, controlled cooling, smoking for reduction
PHOTO BY CINDY YEH

Pamela Wood
Up into the Silence | 2009
120 X 48 X 12 INCHES (304.8 X 121.9 X 30.5 CM)
Hand-built Standard Raku, brushed glaze, carved, sgraffito, oxide wash, gas fired, smoking for reduction
PHOTO BY ARTIST

Richard Lawson
Horsehair Raku | 2009
8¾ X 11 X 11 INCHES (22.2 X 27.9 X 27.9 CM)
Wheel-thrown Laguna B-Mix with grog, sprayed ferric chloride, horsehair, gas fired, controlled cooling
PHOTO BY ARTIST

James Robert Feige
Untitled | 2009
10½ X 7 INCHES (26.7 X 17.8 CM)
Wheel-thrown Soldate, sprayed glaze, electric
fired, alcohol reduction, slow controlled cooling
PHOTO BY JOHN BASSETTO

Frank James Fisher
Relationship Solvent | 2009

7¾ x 4 x 1¼ INCHES (19.7 X 10.2 X 3.2 CM)

Hand-built and slab-built porcelain, image transfer, stamped, underglaze brushwork, gas fired, quick smoking, cone 06

PHOTO BY ARTIST

Travis Winters
Nebula | 2009
10 x 7½ x 7 INCHES (25.4 x 19.1 x 17.8 CM)
Wheel-thrown, altered, and hand-built personal-recipe raku, brushed glaze, gas fired, smoking for reduction, sprayed with water
PHOTO BY ARTIST

Emily E. Ferrell
Untitled | 2009

5½ X 16¾ X 21 INCHES (14 X 42.5 X 53.3 CM)
Hand-built personal-recipe clay, poured and brushed glaze, gas fired, smoking for reduction
PHOTO BY JUAN GRANADOS

Inna Razmakhova
Alive | 2007

11 X 6 X 6 INCHES (27.9 X 15.2 X 15.2 CM)

Wheel-thrown, relief sculpted, and curved B-Mix Stoneware, brushed glaze, terra sigillata, overglaze brushwork, gas fired, smoking for reduction

PHOTO BY ARTIST

Donna Cole
Crosscurrents Teapot | 2008

11½ X 9 X 8 INCHES (29.2 X 22.9 X 20.3 CM)

Tossed and hand-built 3 Finger Jack Stoneware, brushed glaze, stretched, propane-fired raku in oxidation

PHOTO BY ARTIST

Reena Dodeja
Bottle of Purity | 2006
13 x 5 x 9 INCHES (33 x 12.7 x 22.9 CM)
Wheel-thrown porcelain, brushed glaze, gold leaf luster, raku fired, smoking for reduction
PHOTO BY ARTIST

Linda Louise Marbach
Primordial I | 2009
18 X 15 X 6½ INCHES (45.7 X 38.1 X 16.5 CM)
Press-molded Standard 245 and paper pulp, brushed slip resist
and glaze, terra sigillata, gas fired, smoking for reduction
PHOTO BY ARTIST

Susan Clare Worley
Immortal Boy King | 2006
11 x 11 x 3½ INCHES (27.9 X 27.9 X 8.9 CM)
Relief-sculpted and hand-built clay, brushed glaze, carved, stamped, gas fired, smoking for reduction
PHOTO BY STUART NAFEY

Chérie Robin Lockett
Carnival Lights | 2008
5¼ x 5½ x 5 INCHES (13.3 X 14 X 12.7 CM)
Wheel-thrown white stoneware, brushed glaze, carved, gas fired, smoking for reduction
PHOTO BY SANDRA BYERS

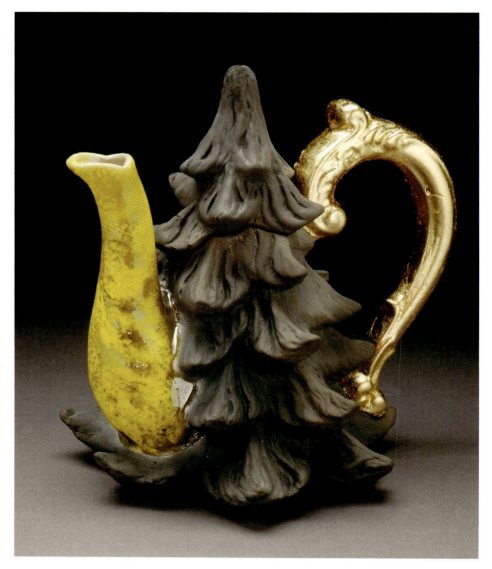

Wesley Eugene Harvey
Christmas Tree Teapot | 2009
6 X 5 X 5 INCHES (15.2 X 12.7 X 12.7 CM)
Slip-cast personal-recipe clay, brushed glaze, gold leaf, non-ceramic/non-fired, gas fired, smoking for reduction, cone 05
PHOTO BY ARTIST

Donna Malson
Zebra Vessel | 2009

11 X 7 X 6 INCHES (27.9 X 17.8 X 15.2 CM)

Thrown, altered, and sculpted cone 10 stoneware, splashed slip and glaze, pop off, terra sigillata, propane fired, naked raku, paper reduction in trash bin, cone 06

PHOTO BY WESLEY HARVEY

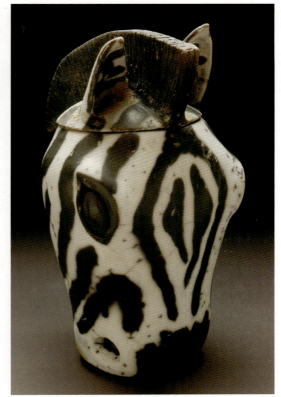

Shuli Pilo
Orange Raku | 2006

8 X 5 X 4 INCHES (20.3 X 12.7 X 10.2 CM)

Hand-built stoneware, brushed glaze, underglaze brushwork, raku fired, smoking for reduction

PHOTO BY ARTIST

Ian F. Thomas
Patrick Whitfill

Because Thumbing the Stars Means Shorter Trees | 2009
4 X 8 X 4 INCHES (10.2 X 20.3 X 10.2 CM)
Hand-built and slab-built clay, brushed glaze,
selective smoking for reduction, cone 03
PHOTO BY ARTISTS

Skip Esquierdo
Crusty Top Pot #2 | 2009
8 X 8 INCHES (20.3 X 20.3 CM)
Wheel-thrown stoneware, sprayed and splashed glaze over patina, propane fired, smoking for reduction
PHOTO BY GLEN ARMAS

Jola Spytkowska
Kettle of Fish | 2008
9 X 8½ X 4½ INCHES (22.9 X 21.6 X 11.4 CM)
Slab-built and hand-built white St. Thomas, brushed glaze, overglaze luster, gas fired, smoking for reduction
PHOTO BY ARTIST

K. Sam Miller
False Idols | 2009
11 X 7 X 6 INCHES (27.9 X 17.8 X 15.2 CM)
Hand-built, pinched, and coiled Trinity Ceramics Grande
Stoneware, brushed glaze, gas fired, smoking for reduction
PHOTO BY HARRISON EVANS

Gerald Hong
Kelly Hong
Bellevue 60 Bell | 2006
26 x 16 x 11 INCHES (66 x 40.6 x 27.9 CM)
Slab-built Laguna WSO, brushed and sprayed glaze, sprigged, stamped, sgraffito, inlaid glaze, gold leaf, gas fired, smoking for reduction
PHOTO BY ARTISTS

Kate Jacobson
Will Jacobson
Koi | 2009

14 X 15 X 15 INCHES (35.6 X 38.1 X 38.1 CM)
Wheel-thrown Laguna WC370, brushed slip, poured glaze, naked raku, gas fired, smoking for reduction

PHOTO BY ARTISTS

Lorraine Sutter
Black Collar | 2009

8 X 6 X 6 INCHES (20.3 X 15.2 X 15.2 CM)

Wheel-thrown porcelain, brushed glaze, slip resist, electric fired, smoking for reduction, cone 012

PHOTO BY ARTIST

Roland Summer
Untitled | 2009

17 11/16 X 13 3/8 X 13 3/8 INCHES (45 X 34 X 34 CM)

Hand-built and burnished grogged white clay, terra sigillata, gas fired, smoking for reduction

PHOTO BY ARTIST

Jane Beall
Sea Urchin | 2009
7 X 18 X 10 INCHES (17.8 X 45.7 X 25.4 CM)
Hand-built stoneware, brushed glaze, gas fired, smoking for reduction
PHOTO BY JOHN OLIVER LEWIS

Maria Antonietta Ciccia
Cenerentola | 2008
9 X 12 X 7 INCHES (22.9 X 30.5 X 17.8 CM)
Hand-built sila clay, naked raku, sgraffito, gas fired, smoking for reduction
PHOTO BY GIAMPAOLO SORGI

Ginny Marsh
Bottle | 2006
5½ X 5½ X 5½ INCHES (14 X 14 X 14 CM)
Wheel-thrown personal-recipe clay, brushed glaze, gas fired, smoking for reduction
PHOTO BY ARTIST

Brian L. Jensen
Double-Lidded Jar | 2009
17 X 10 X 10 INCHES (43.2 X 25.4 X 25.4 CM)
Thrown and altered personal-recipe clay, brushed glaze, gas fired, smoking for reduction, cone 04
PHOTO BY ARTIST

David P. Parr
Energy Burst | 2008

12 X 14 INCHES (30.5 X 35.6 CM)

Hand-built and slab-built personal-recipe clay, brushed glaze, carved, gas fired, smoking for reduction

PHOTO BY FRANK JAMES FISHER

Jake R. Allee
Incised Jar | 2009

6½ X 5 X 5 INCHES (16.5 X 12.7 X 12.7 CM)

Thrown and incised personal-recipe clay, sprayed glaze, carved, gas fired, smoking for reduction, quick cooling

PHOTO BY ARTIST

Sigal Vaisgur
Human Fish | 2009

5½ X 11 X 4⁵⁄₁₆ INCHES (14 X 27.9 X 11 CM)
Hand-built Sibelco K129, brushed glaze, gas fired, smoking for reduction
PHOTO BY ILAN AMIHAI

Pete Wysong
Armadillo Dreaming | 2007
12 x 9 x 14 INCHES (30.5 x 22.9 x 35.6 CM)
Thrown and altered Mile Hi 2002 Raku, brushed glaze, terra sigillata, carved, stamped, gas fired, smoking for reduction, cone 08
PHOTO BY ARTIST

Paul R. Harp
Abbott and Costello | 2009
TALLEST: 8 X 6¼ X 6¼ INCHES (20.3 X 15.9 X 15.9 CM)
Wheel-thrown Miller Raku, dipped and poured glaze, slip resist, gas fired, selective smoking for reduction, buried in hardwood sawdust layers, bisque fired, cone 03
PHOTO BY ARTIST

Jerel M. Harwood
Descent | 2009
6 X 8 X 14 INCHES (15.2 X 20.3 X 35.6 CM)
Coiled earthenware, brushed vitreous engobe, sgraffito, gas fired, smoking for reduction, cone 03
PHOTO BY ARTIST

Susan Halls
Ornamental Horse and Rider | 2008

9 X 7 X 3½ INCHES (22.9 X 17.8 X 8.9 CM)

Press-molded, thrown, and altered personal-recipe paper clay, poured colloidal slip, electric fired, selective smoking for reduction

PHOTO BY JOHN POLAK

Fred Yokel
How'd This Happen? | 2007
26 x 9 x 8 INCHES (66 x 22.9 x 20.3 CM)
Coil-built Clay Planet Sculpture Raku, brushed and sponged glaze and underglaze, scraped, carved, gas fired, post-firing sawdust reduction, cone 08
PHOTO BY ARTIST

Yasmine Redding
Desert Lidded Jar | 2008

11 X 7½ X 7½ INCHES (27.9 X 19.1 X 19.1 CM)

Wheel-thrown Vegas Buff Stoneware, brushed glaze, gas fired, sprayed with ferric chloride, reduction with paper, slow cooling

PHOTO BY ARTIST

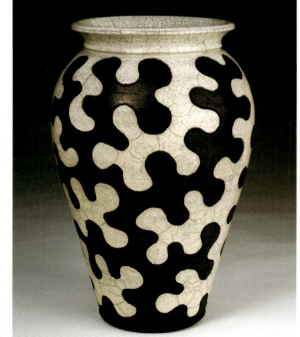

Lance Andrew Timco
Puzzle Pot with White Crackle Glaze | 2007

18 X 9 X 9 INCHES (45.7 X 22.9 X 22.9 CM)

Wheel-thrown and carved recycled scrap, brushed glaze, carved, gas-fired raku, heavy reduction

PHOTO BY ARTIST

Richard Anthony Moren
Blue India | 2008
24 × 22 × 20 INCHES (61 × 55.9 × 50.8 CM)
Thrown and coiled Bruce's Raku, brushed glaze, carved, propane fired, reduction, cold-water quick cooling
PHOTO BY ARTIST

Chris Vivas
Hollowmen: Series I | 2005
6 X 3 X 2½ INCHES (15.2 X 7.6 X 6.4 CM)
Hand-built Standard 236 Raku, brushed glaze, raku fired, quick cooling in water
PHOTO BY ARTIST

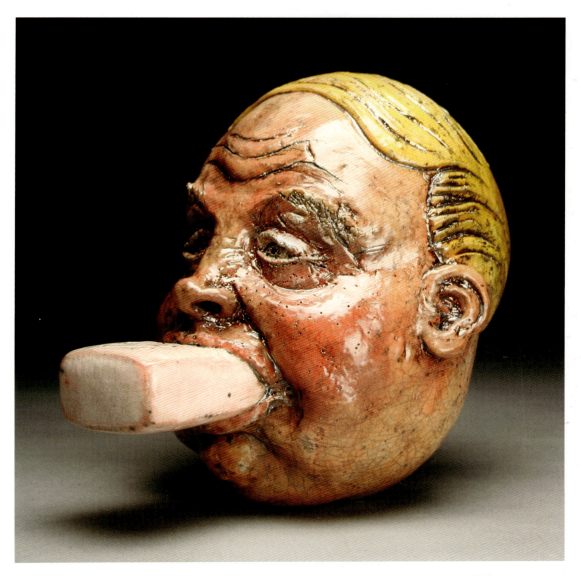

Eric John Nauman
Potty Mouth | 2009
9½ X 8 X 10½ INCHES (24.1 X 20.3 X 26.7 CM)
Hand-built white raku, brushed and sponged glaze, underglaze brushwork, oxide wash, overglazed, gas fired, quick smoking
PHOTO BY ERIC HCEFFUR

Falina Sinopah Lintner
Untitled | 2009

15 X 14 X 3 INCHES (38.1 X 35.6 X 7.6 CM)
Press-molded and hand-built personal-recipe clay, brushed glaze, carved, gas fired, smoking for reduction
PHOTO BY ARTIST

Laura O'Donnell
Shadows | 2009
9 X 7¼ X 2 INCHES (22.9 X 18.4 X 5.1 CM)
Hand-built and slab-built personal-recipe clay, brushed glaze, carved, modeled, gas fired, smoking for reduction
PHOTO BY ARTIST

Teresa Testa
Shimmer | 2009
7 x 10 x 6 INCHES (17.8 x 25.4 x 15.2 CM)
Hand-built Aardvark Raku White, brushed glaze, dremel carved, hand formed, quick cooling in water, limited reduction
PHOTO BY ARTIST

Stef Greener
Night Sky Vessel | 2009
9½ × 6¾ INCHES (24.1 × 17.1 CM)
Wheel-thrown Laguna Steve's White, brushed and splashed glaze, propane fired, smoking for reduction
PHOTO BY BILL GREENER

Tom Mahaffey
Flame On | 2009
16 × 8 × 5 INCHES (40.6 × 20.3 × 12.7 CM)
Hand-built and slab-built Great Lakes Raku III, sprayed and poured glaze, gas fired, smoking for reduction
PHOTO BY ARTIST

Lori Lee Dudley
Queen of the World | 2009
12 X 6 X 5 INCHES (30.5 X 15.2 X 12.7 CM)
Thrown and altered personal-recipe clay, brushed glaze, engobe brushwork, gas fired, smoking for reduction
PHOTO BY DAN DUDLEY

Marijke Janssen
Listening | 2008
25 9/16 X 9 13/16 INCHES (65 X 25 CM)
Hand-built paper clay, brushed glaze, gas fired
PHOTO BY EDWARD LOOS

Molly I. Brauhn
Time Travel (Vehicle I) | 2009
24 X 8 X 9 INCHES (61 X 20.3 X 22.9 CM)
Hand and slab-built cone 6 clay, brushed glaze, underglaze brushwork and pencils, electric and gas fired, quick smoking, smoking for reduction
PHOTO BY ARTIST

Kevin Arthur Myers
Rushmore | 2008
16 X 16 X 14 INCHES (40.6 X 40.6 X 35.6 CM)
Thrown, altered, and sculpted Laguna K, brushed, poured, and sprayed glaze, torn, pierced, paddled, gas fired, quick smoking, selective smoking for reduction
PHOTO BY ANTHONY CUNHA

Karen Gail Adelaar
Astral Image II | 2008
10 X 10 INCHES (25.4 X 25.4 CM)
Hand-built porcelain, terra sigillata slips, carved, black walnut wash, gas fired, quick smoking, selective smoking for reduction
PHOTO BY STEPHEN I. GLUCK

Cac Ninh
Dao De Jing (Chapter 11) | 2008
10 X 8½ X 8 INCHES (25.4 X 21.6 X 20.3 CM)
Wheel-thrown Babu Porcelain, brushed glaze, acrylic resist, tape resist, gas-fired raku, controlled cooling, quick smoking
PHOTO BY ARTIST

Eunice Bridges
Reforestation | 2009

9 X 13 X 9 INCHES (22.9 X 33 X 22.9 CM)

Wheel-thrown and altered raku clay, brushed porcelain slip and glaze, oxide detailing, gas fired, heavy reduction in newspaper and sawdust

PHOTO BY ARTIST

Sam Scott
Lidded Jar | 2008
7½ X 5 X 5 INCHES (19.1 X 12.7 X 12.7 CM)
Wheel-thrown Scott Stoneware, poured alligator glaze, propane fired, smoking for reduction, controlled cooling, cone 06
PHOTO BY ARTIST

Judy Bolef Miller
Ready to Play | 2007
8½ X 9½ X 6 INCHES (21.6 X 24.1 X 15.2 CM)
Hand-built Imco Sculpture Mix 412,
electric and gas fired, smoking for reduction
PHOTO BY ARTIST

Dan Dudley
Mariachi | 2008

36 X 60 X 10 INCHES (91.4 X 152.4 X 25.4 CM)

Hand-built personal-recipe clay, brushed glaze, engobe brushwork, gas fired, smoking for reduction

PHOTOS BY ARTIST

Ariella Anderson
Ignite | 2005

31 1/2 X 20 1/16 X 4 5/16 INCHES (80 X 51 X 11 CM)

Slab-built, textured, and shaped Walker White Raku, sprayed and poured glaze, imprinted, electric fired, smoking for reduction

PHOTO BY PETER SPARGO

Katherine Dube
Overflow | 2005
10 X 7 X 7 INCHES (25.4 X 17.8 X 17.8 CM)
Wheel-thrown stoneware, dipped glaze, gas fired, controlled cooling
PHOTO BY ARTIST

Susan Yamaguchi
Copper Matt Raku | 2009

6 X 8¼ X 25½ INCHES (15.2 X 21 X 64.8 CM)

Wheel-thrown Soldate 60, sprayed glaze, gas fired, sprayed with rubbing alcohol, reduction in chamber with pine needles, sprayed with water for cooling

PHOTO BY DANIEL FORKIN

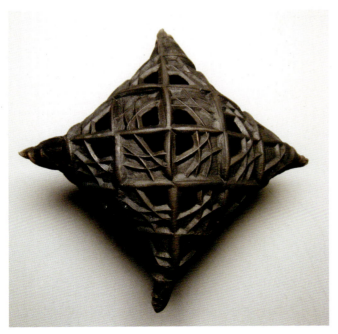

Bob Miranti
Gothic Cross | 2007

6 X 6 X 4 INCHES (15.2 X 15.2 X 10.2 CM)

Hand-built stoneware, unglazed, carved, stamped, gas fired, smoking for reduction

PHOTO BY ARTIST

Lisa Marie Booe
Touch Me Not | 2008
20 X 24 X 6 INCHES (50.8 X 61 X 15.2 CM)
Hand-built and slab-built raku, brushed glaze, carved, slips, underglazes, gas-fired raku, post-fire reduction
PHOTO BY LENNY DOWHIE

Sally Aldrich
Flock: White Crackle Birds | 2009
EACH: 6 X 10 X 4 INCHES (15.2 X 25.4 X 10.2 CM)
Relief-sculpted and hand-built buff stoneware, brushed glaze, carved, raku fired
PHOTO BY HOWARD GOODMAN

Kate Missett
Ganesh Jar | 2008
18 X 8 X 6 INCHES (45.7 X 20.3 X 15.2 CM)
Wheel-thrown and hand-built Standard S239, poured, brushed, and splashed glazes, raku fired, smoking in organic material, immersed in water
PHOTO BY D. JAMES DEE

Tomoko Amaki Abe
Twelve Moons | 2008
36 X 36 X 5 INCHES (91.4 X 91.4 X 12.7 CM)
Slab-built raku, brushed and sprayed glaze, screen-printed, overglazed, electric fired, quick cooling in water, smoking for reduction
PHOTO BY HOWARD GOODMAN

Sandy Ashbaugh

From the *Swirl Series* | 2009

7½ X 5 X 2¼ INCHES (19.1 X 12.7 X 5.7 CM)

Hand-built cone 5 white stoneware, brushed glaze, stamped, carved, gas fired in top-hat kiln, quick removal, post-reduction in garbage can with newspaper, cone 06

PHOTO BY ARTIST

Colleen Sweeney Gahrmann
Raku Vessel II | 2006
6 X 7 X 8 INCHES (15.2 X 17.8 X 20.3 CM)
Wheel-thrown Standard Clay, poured glaze, propane fired, smoking for reduction
PHOTO BY RICH VOGEL

JoLea S. Arcidiacono
Haeckel Spiral | 2009
8½ X 9 X 8 INCHES (21.6 X 22.9 X 20.3 CM)
Hand-built Armadillo Raku, brushed glaze, gas fired, smoking for reduction
PHOTO BY ARTIST

Deanna Lee Bourke
Untitled | 2008

6 X 4 X 4 INCHES (15.2 X 10.2 X 10.2 CM)
Wheel-thrown B-Mix, terra sigillata, burnished, gas-fired saggar in reduction, horsehair raku
PHOTO BY JOHN OLIVER LEWIS

Katrina Mae Florell
Security | 2008

46 X 36 X 8 INCHES (116.8 X 91.4 X 20.3 CM)
Press-molded and slab-built raku, sprayed glaze, carved, electric fired, smoking for reduction

PHOTOS BY BAER PHOTOGRAPHY

Dawn Whitehand
Hillside | 2006
9 X 11 X 4 INCHES (22.9 X 27.9 X 10.2 CM)
Slab-built personal-recipe clay, brushed glaze, gas fired, smoking for reduction, quick cooling in water
PHOTO BY ARTIST

Kay Alliband
Mothers' Angels | 2008
8 X 2½ X 3 INCHES (20.3 X 6.4 X 7.6 CM) EACH
Hand-built, thrown, and altered Keane's White Raku, brushed glaze, underglaze brushwork, luster, gas fired, smoking for reduction
PHOTO BY COLIN HUSBAND

Natasha Elizabeth Corbett
Moon Crater | 2008
18 X 3½ INCHES (45.7 X 8.9 CM)
Press-molded Keane's White Raku, brushed and sponged glaze, stamped, gas fired, smoking for reduction, quick cooling in water
PHOTO BY ARTIST

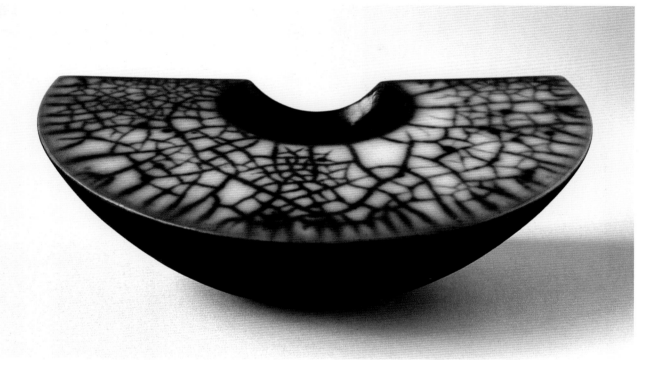

Emma Johnstone
Medium Segment | 2006
3½ X 9 X 8 INCHES (8.9 X 22.9 X 20.3 CM)
Thrown and altered Scarva Professional White Raku, brushed glaze, naked raku, burnished, waxed, gas fired, smoking for reduction
PHOTO BY JAMES WADDELL

Ri Van Veen
Web of Life | 2008
17 x 12 x 8 INCHES (43.2 x 30.5 x 20.3 CM)
Hand-built, slab-built, and coiled red raku, gas fired, smoking for reduction
PHOTO BY SIMON FOX

Ruth Gilad
Naked Raku Jar | 2007
12 9/16 x 9 13/16 x 9 13/16 INCHES (31.9 x 24.9 x 24.9 CM)
Wheel-thrown K-123, terra sigillata, bisque fired, dipped in iron salt and slip, reduction in sawdust, submerged in water post-firing
PHOTO BY ARTIST

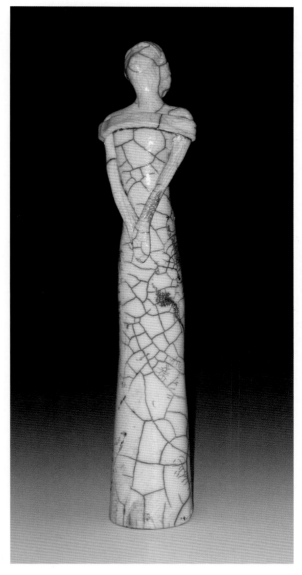

Sherry Dresser
Untitled | 2009

15 X 3 X 2¾ INCHES (38.1 X 7.6 X 7 CM)

Slab-built and hand-built Pottery Supply House 515
Stoneware, brushed glaze, gas fired, cone 06

PHOTO BY ARTIST

Ariella Anderson
Pieces of Me | 2006
22 13/16 X 15 5/16 X 5 1/2 INCHES (58 X 39 X 14 CM)
Hand-built and slab-built Walker White Raku, sprayed glaze, imprinted with gold non-fired finish, electric fired, controlled cooling, smoking for reduction
PHOTO BY STEWART RIDDLE

Colette Beardall
Days Gone By | 2006
6 X 3 X 2½ INCHES (15.2 X 7.6 X 6.4 CM)
Sculpted Tucker's Sculpture Clay, brushed glaze, propane-fired raku, heavy sawdust and newspaper reduction
PHOTO BY ARTIST

Thelma Marie Howard
Wave Crest | 2009
10 X 10½ X 8½ INCHES (25.4 X 26.7 X 21.6 CM)
Hand-built, press-molded, and coiled Plainsman 441 G, dipped glaze, stamped, propane fired, quick reduction, quick cooling in water
PHOTO BY L. SUTTER

Amourentia Louisa Leibman
Treasure Keeper | 2008
6 X 6 X 4½ INCHES (15.2 X 15.2 X 11.4 CM)
Slab-built WSO Laguna cone 10, brushed and dipped glaze, sprigged, stamped, press molded, gas-fired raku, smoking for reduction, cone 06

PHOTO BY ARTIST

Dainis Lesins
Vase with Zigzag Lines | 2009

11 3/16 X 7 1/16 INCHES (28.4 X 17.9 CM)

Wheel-thrown raku clay with grog, sponged glaze, carved, gas fired, smoking for reduction, seger cone 04a

PHOTO BY ARTIST

Leticia Garcia
Fire Dance | 2008

10 9/16 X 7 1/2 X 7 1/2 INCHES (26.8 X 19.1 X 19.1 CM)

Hand-built personal-recipe clay, brushed glaze, oxide wash, gas fired, smoking for reduction, cone 07

PHOTO BY ALEX STRAUBE

Keiko Matsui
Shikaku Raku | 2006
EACH: 6½ X 6½ X 1⁹⁄₁₆ INCHES (16.5 X 16.5 X 4 CM)
Hand-built and slab-built personal-recipe clay, dipped glaze, on-glaze brushwork, gas fired, quick cooling in water
PHOTO BY LIOR EHUD

Mori Yamauchi
Untitled | 2009
TALLEST: 11 ½ X 2 X 2 INCHES (29.2 X 5.1 X 5.1 CM)
Hand-built and slab-built raku, dipped glaze, carved, faceted, gas fired, smoking for reduction
PHOTO BY ARTIST

Lillian Forester
Overseer | 2009
7¼ x 4¼ x 3¾ INCHES (18.4 X 10.8 X 9.5 CM)
Wheel-thrown PSH Raku, brushed glaze,
gas-fired raku, smoking for reduction
PHOTO BY DALE RODDICK

Sarah Beck
Love Puffins | 2009
10 X 10 X 5 INCHES (25.4 X 25.4 X 12.7 CM)
Hand-built Tucker's White Sculpture Clay, brushed glaze, impressed, electric fired, cooled, smoked
PHOTO BY ARTIST

Yola Vale Resende
Untitled | 2006

2½ X 16 X 16 INCHES (6.4 X 40.6 X 40.6 CM)
Relief-sculpted and hand-built CH-B, Vicente Diez commercial clay, brushed glaze, carved, overglaze, terra sigillata, gas fired, smoking for reduction

PHOTO BY ARTIST

Elaine Rasmussen
Naked Raku Vessel | 2006

7 X 6 INCHES (17.8 X 15.2 CM)
Wheel-thrown Soldate 60, poured glaze, splashed slip, gas fired, smoking for reduction, slip removal

PHOTO BY JON BISCHOFFBERGER

Nina Hole
Modul System | 2009
9 X 4 X 3 FEET (2.7 X 1.2 X 0.9 M)
Slab-built, terra sigillatas, wood fired
PHOTOS BY ARTIST

Nina Hope Pfanstiehl
African Princess | 2009

14 X 3¼ X 2¾ INCHES (35.6 X 8.3 X 7 CM)
Hand-built Miller #250 Raku, brushed glaze, underglaze, electric fired, propane fired, smoking for reduction

PHOTO BY ARTIST

Vilma Villaverde
Lantern | 2006

27½ X 9½ X 8 INCHES (69.9 X 24.1 X 20.3 CM)
Hand-built commercial clay, sprayed glaze, electric fired, smoking for reduction, controlled cooling

PHOTO BY JOSE CRISTELLI

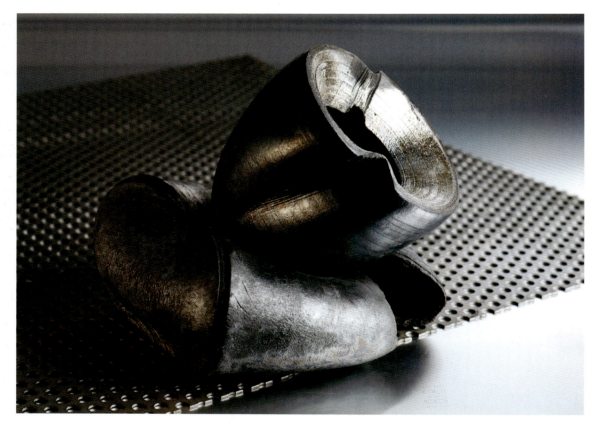

David Jones
Broken Hearted | 2007
13 x 17 x 12 INCHES (33 X 43.2 X 30.5 CM)
Thrown and altered T material, sprayed glaze, gas fired, smoking for reduction
PHOTO BY ROD DORLING

Gise Trauttmansdorff
Voyage | 2008
LONGEST: 16 INCHES (40.6 CM)
Slab-built Tucker's Sculpture Clay, sprayed glaze, propane fired, quick smoking
PHOTO BY ARTIST

Cordula Bielenstein-Morich
Coming | 2009
27 X 48 X 48 INCHES (68.6 X 121.9 X 121.9 CM)
Thrown and altered Cebex W2505, sprayed glaze, carved, pushed, gas fired, smoking for reduction
PHOTO BY ARTIST

Karen Mahoney
Hokusai Teabowl | 2009
4 X 4½ X 4½ INCHES (10.2 X 11.4 X 11.4 CM)
Wheel-thrown Laguna 10T, brushed glaze, carved,
underglaze brushwork, propane fired, smoking for reduction
PHOTO BY ARTIST

Cathy M. Harris
Snow-Covered Sphere with Tree | 2008
5½ X 4 X 12 INCHES (14 X 10.2 X 30.5 CM)
Wheel-thrown Tucker's Porcelain, dipped glaze, gas fired, selective smoking for reduction, controlled reduction
PHOTO BY NAT CARON

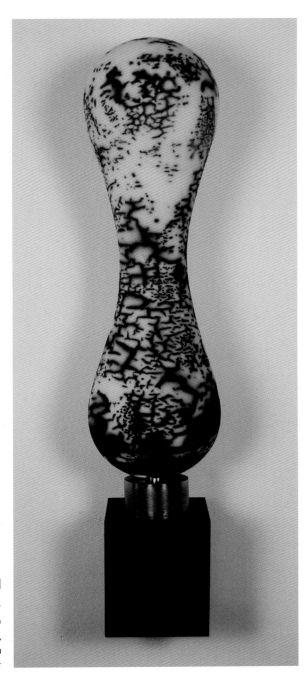

Gale McCall
Untitled | 2008
13 X 4 INCHES (33 X 10.2 CM)
Slip-cast Laguna Toshi, naked raku, brushed slip,
gas fired, newspaper smoking for reduction
PHOTO BY ARTIST

Gerri Orwin
Red Planet | 2009

12 X 4 X 4 INCHES (30.5 X 10.2 X 10.2 CM)

Hand-built, slab-built, and coiled Thompson Raku, sprayed glaze, stamped, salts, moss, ferric chloride, aluminum foil, gas-fired raku, smoking for reduction

PHOTO BY JACK GRAHAM

Catherine Weir
Shadow Crackle Trefoil Bowl | 2008
7 X 9 INCHES (17.8 X 22.9 CM)

Wheel-thrown Sheba Raku, brushed and poured glaze, tape resist, propane-fired raku, controlled cooling, smoking for reduction

PHOTO BY CHRISTIE GRUPPE

Gale Lurie
Double-Spouted Vase | 2007
9 X 9½ X 1¾ INCHES (22.9 X 24.1 X 4.4 CM)

Press-molded, wheel-thrown, and hand-built Mt. Baker White with grog, dipped glaze, scratched, propane-fired bisque, smoking for reduction

PHOTO BY ARTIST

Nurit Dreizin
Looking Forward | 2007
6½ X 5½ X 7 INCHES (16.5 X 14 X 17.8 CM)
Hand-built and coiled clay, sprayed glaze, gas fired, quick smoking
PHOTO BY REFAEL DRYZIN

Jo Priestley
Forest Fossil Lidded Urn 1 | 2008
14½ x 7½ INCHES (36.8 X 19.1 CM)
Wheel-thrown Clay Art Hutchins Raku, brushed slip,
sprayed glaze, glued fern, gas fired, smoking for reduction
PHOTO BY GORAN BASARIC

500 RAKU

Christopher Reid Flock
Untitled | 2008
22 X 7 INCHES (55.9 X 17.8 CM)
Thrown, altered, and hand-built PSH Raku, dipped and sprayed glaze, stamped, gas fired, quick reduction, quick cooling with water
PHOTO BY ARTIST

Jack Lin
Untitled | 2009
5 INCHES (13 CM) TALL
Wheel-thrown sculpture soil, dipped glaze, raku fired, quick cooling in water, smoking for reduction
PHOTO BY ARTIST

Biliana Popova
Large Raku Bowl | 2009
7 X 18 INCHES (17.8 X 45.7 CM)
Coil-built stoneware, brushed glaze, tape resist, raku fired, smoking for reduction
PHOTO BY ARTIST

Julie C. Hilliard
Raku Vessel | 2009

8 X 8 X 2½ INCHES (20.3 X 20.3 X 6.4 CM)
Hand-built and slab-built Highwater Raku, dipped glaze, wax-resist brushwork, gas fired, smoking for reduction, newspaper combustible
PHOTO BY WALKER MONTGOMERY

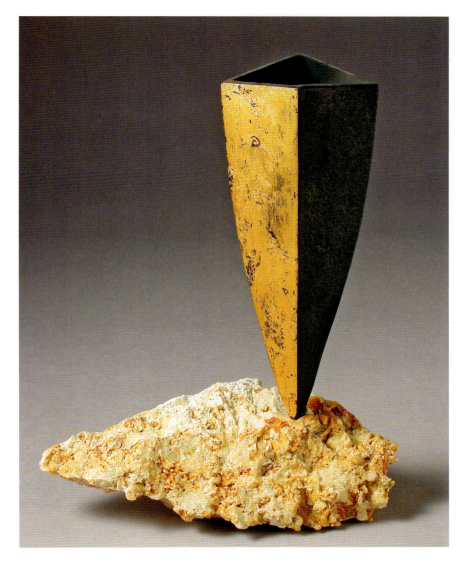

Michael Sheba
Icon Series 2 | 2007
7½ X 6 X 3 INCHES (19.1 X 15.2 X 7.6 CM)
Hand-built and assembled PSH Sheba Raku with fossilized stone, burnished, sgraffito, 24-karat gold leaf, propane-fired raku, smoking for reduction, cone 06
PHOTO BY ARTIST

Frank James Fisher
Syngas Tea-Can | 2009
7 X 6 X 5 INCHES (17.8 X 15.2 X 12.7 CM)
Hand-built, slab-built, and wheel-thrown porcelain, brushed, sponged, poured, and splashed glaze, washed, stenciled, gas fired, controlled cooling, selective smoking for reduction, shredded ink paper, sawdust
PHOTO BY ARTIST

Sharon Faktorowich
Tranquility | 2008
40 × 8 INCHES (101.6 × 20.3 CM)
Relief-sculpted and slab-built K129, brushed glaze, screen-printed, electric fired, smoking for reduction
PHOTO BY SUZANNE LAUTERBACH

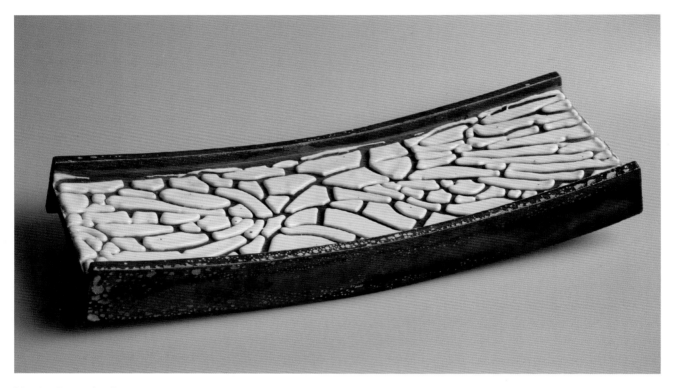

Karin Putsch-Grassi
Iron Girder | 2009

2½ X 12½ X 4½ INCHES (6.4 X 31.8 X 11.4 CM)

Slab-built personal-recipe clay, brushed and poured glaze, gas fired, reduction with sawdust

PHOTO BY ARTIST

Jadranka Rukavina
My Childhood | 2005
4 X 1 X 6 INCHES (10.2 X 2.5 X 15.2 CM)
Hand-built commercial raku, brushed glaze, overglazed, electric fired, smoking for reduction
PHOTO BY BORIS PLESA

Birgitta Frazier
Stormy Night | 2007
16½ X 7⅞ INCHES (42 X 20 CM)
Stoneware, raku fired
PHOTO BY ARTIST

Mark Lusardi
Wind Walker | 2008
17 X 20 INCHES (43.2 X 50.8 CM)
Slab-built, wheel-thrown, and altered Continental Raku, brushed, dipped, and poured glaze, carved, slip trailed, gas fired, heavy reduction
PHOTO BY MIKE JENSEN PHOTOGRAPHY

Peter Wirun
Thespian | 2008
16 x 5½ x 3¾ INCHES (40.6 X 14 X 9.5 CM)
Relief-sculpted and hand-built Thompson Raku, dipped glaze, head unglazed, gas fired, quick cooling in water, smoking for reduction
PHOTO BY SANDRA WIRUN

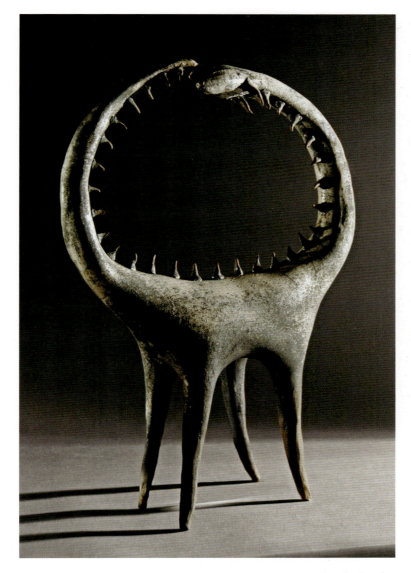

Barb Sachs
Biter | 2009
14 x 12 x 4 INCHES (35.6 X 30.5 X 10.2 CM)
Hand-built Tucker's White Sculpture Clay, sprayed glaze, gas fired, smoking for reduction
PHOTO BY JAMES CHAMBERS

Kate Jacobson
Will Jacobson
Tropical Dream | 2009
11 X 12 X 12 INCHES (27.9 X 30.5 X 30.5 CM)
Thrown and altered Laguna WC370, brushed slip, poured glaze, naked raku, gas fired, smoking for reduction
PHOTO BY ARTISTS

Gerald Hong
Kelly Hong
Undulating Vessel with Iris | 2008
14 X 9 X 4 INCHES (35.6 X 22.9 X 10.2 CM)
Slab-built Laguna WSO, brushed and sprayed glaze, stamped, sgraffito, inlaid glaze, gold leaf, gas fired, smoking for reduction
PHOTO BY ARTISTS

Bob Green
Melon Globe | 2006

12 X 14 X 14 INCHES (30.5 X 35.6 X 35.6 CM)

Thrown Sheffield S14, sprayed glaze, multiple glaze firings, gas fired, reduced with damp wood chips, cone 06

PHOTO BY KEN BURRIS

JoAnn F. Axford
Poppy-Covered Jar | 2005
11 ½ X 8 ½ X 8 ½ INCHES (29.2 X 21.6 X 21.6 CM)
Wheel-thrown Laguna/Miller #66, brushed and poured glaze, sgraffito, gas fired, top hat raku, smoking for reduction
PHOTO BY ARTIST

Anthony E. Stellaccio
Roofed Vessel | 2007
8½ X 12 X 6 INCHES (21.6 X 30.5 X 15.2 CM)
Slab-built commercial earthenware, brushed glaze, resist decorated, wood fired, smoking for reduction
PHOTO BY ARTIST

Lambeth Walker Marshall
Landscape Pot 3 | 2009

8 X 10¼ X 4 INCHES (20.3 X 26 X 10.2 CM)

Slab-built Highwater Raku, sprayed underglazes, poured glazes, raku top hat propane fired

PHOTO BY ARTIST

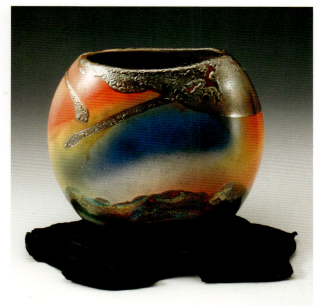

Irina Clopatofsky Velasco
Waterfall | 2007

5 X 5½ INCHES (12.7 X 14 CM)

Thrown, altered, and cut Miller Clay #200, brushed glaze, carved, gas fired, reduction, cooled with water

PHOTO BY RYAN FLATHAU

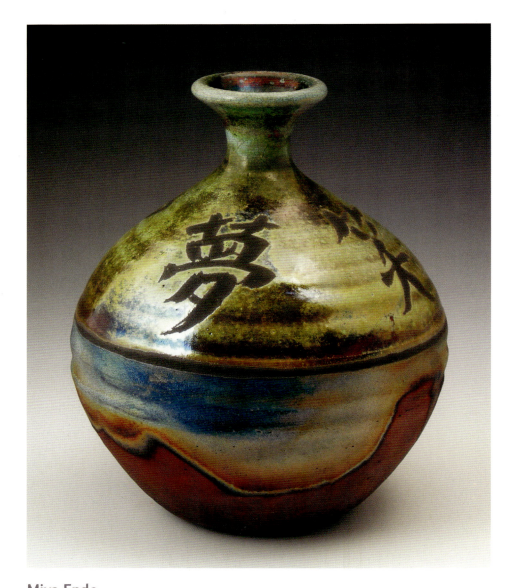

Miya Endo
Untitled | 2008
6 X 5 X 5 INCHES (15.2 X 12.7 X 12.7 CM)
Wheel-thrown New Mexico High Hills Clay, dipped glaze, wax resist, gas fired, controlled cooling, smoking for reduction, cone 06
PHOTO BY ARTIST

Gina Mars
Ritual Vessel | 2009
12 X 9 X 9 INCHES (30.5 X 22.9 X 22.9 CM)
Wheel thrown and altered 239 Standard Raku Clay, sprayed and brushed glaze, stamped, carved, extruded, raku fired in propane kiln, alcohol reduction, reduction in sawdust
PHOTO BY ARTIST

Teri Hannigan
Shinji Vase | 2007

10 X 5 X 5 INCHES (25.4 X 12.7 X 12.7 CM)

Wheel-thrown, carved, and altered Laguna B-Mix, brushed glazes, stamped, gas fired, selective smoking for reduction

PHOTO BY ANTHONY CUNHA

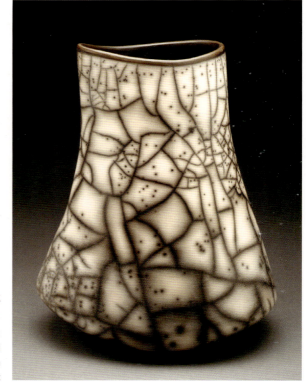

Janine Parent
Untitled | 2005

17 X 14 INCHES (43.2 X 35.6 CM)

Coil built PSH Sheba Raku, poured slip and glaze, gas fired, smoking for reduction

PHOTO BY GUY COUTURE

Liz Pasenow
Wheel-Thrown Vessel with Lid | 2008
9 X 8 X 5 INCHES (22.9 X 20.3 X 12.7 CM)
Wheel-thrown and sculpted Sheba Raku, brushed terra sigillata and glaze, carved, sgraffito, propane fired, quick cooling in water, smoking for reduction
PHOTO BY SHEILA CLENNELL

Shari Bray
Ibis | 2009

11 3/8 X 10 INCHES (28.9 X 25.4 CM)

Slab-built Aardvark Raku White, brushed glaze, overglaze, raku fired, reduction in sawdust and newspaper

PHOTO BY ARTIST

Deborah Johnston
Untitled | 2008
14 X 5 X 3 INCHES (35.6 X 12.7 X 7.6 CM)
Slab-built stoneware, brushed glaze, gas fired, smoking
PHOTO BY ARTIST

Jim Connell
Green Carved Oval Bottle | 2005

7 X 7 X 3 INCHES (17.8 X 17.8 X 7.6 CM)

Thrown, paddled, and carved stoneware/raku, sprayed glaze, electric fired, quick smoking, smoking for reduction, cone 06

PHOTO BY ARTIST

Philippe A. Buraud
Untitled | 2008

14 X 3¼ INCHES (35.6 X 8.3 CM)

Wheel-thrown Finegrog Stoneware, Solargil Raku Mitsu, no glaze, brushed terra sigillata, gas fired, smoking for reduction

PHOTO BY ARTIST

Emily Jo Lees
Untitled | 2008
2½ X 7 X 7 INCHES (6.4 X 17.8 X 17.8 CM)
Slab-built Highwater Raku, brushed glaze, underglaze brushwork,
gas-fired raku, smoking for reduction, 1850°F (1010°C)
PHOTO BY SETH TICE-LEWIS

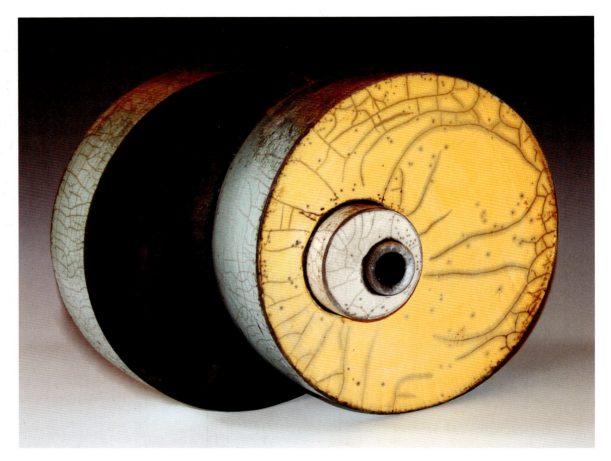

Michael Lancaster
Disc One Disc Two | 2009
14 X 20 X 10 INCHES (35.6 X 50.8 X 25.4 CM)
Thrown, altered, and assembled Laguna Big White Stoneware, brushed glaze, underglaze brushwork, overglaze, gas fired, smoking for reduction in straw
PHOTO BY ARTIST

Monica Litvany
Vessel | 2008
13½ X 8½ X 7 INCHES (34.3 X 21.6 X 17.8 CM)
Hand-built Laguna #250 Raku, brushed glaze, terra sigillata, gas fired, smoking for reduction
PHOTO BY PETER JACOBS

Judy Geerts
Girl with Raku Vessel | 2008
30 X 22 X 17 INCHES (76.2 X 55.9 X 43.2 CM)
Hand-built, slab-built, and pinched Great Lakes Smooth Raku, brushed and sprayed glaze, carved, stamped, controlled cooling
PHOTO BY PAT CHAMBERS

Lisa Merida-Paytes
Earth Stack Series: Proof | 2007
84 X 76 X 73 INCHES (213.4 X 193 X 185.4 CM)
Hand-built and slab-built Columbus Raku, brushed and dipped glaze, carved, stamped, overglazed, gas fired, controlled cooling, selective smoking for reduction, cone 05
PHOTO BY JAY BACHEMIN

George Tomkins
Tea Bowl | 2009

4½ X 5½ X 5½ INCHES (11.4 X 14 X 14 CM)

Thrown and altered WSO Laguna, brushed glaze, gas fired, selective smoking for reduction

PHOTO BY ARTIST

Steven Branfman
Teabowl | 2009

3 X 4 INCHES (7.6 X 10.2 CM)

Thrown and altered Laguna #250, brushed and poured glaze, pressed texture, propane fired, controlled cooling with water spray, reduction in wood shavings

PHOTO BY ARTIST

Penny Truitt
Arch II | 2005
23 X 6 X 12 INCHES (58.4 X 15.2 X 30.5 CM)
Slab-built personal-recipe clay, sprayed glaze,
oxide wash, gas fired, smoking for reduction
PHOTO BY CHRIS STEWART

Rhonda Gushee
The Thinking Cap | 2005

22 X 12 X 8 INCHES (55.9 X 30.5 X 20.3 CM)

Press-molded, hand-built, and altered Columbus White Raku, brushed glaze, carved, underglaze brushwork, electric fired, smoking for reduction, cone 04

PHOTO BY JAY BACHEMIN

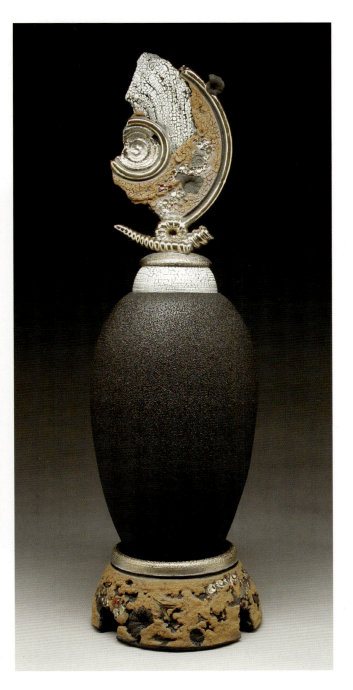

Sheldon Ganstrom
Jaguar Vessel | 2009
26 X 7 X 7 INCHES (66 X 17.8 X 17.8 CM)
Wheel-thrown, thrown, and altered white stoneware with kyanite, brushed glaze and engobes, overglazed, electric fired, heavy reduction, cone 06
PHOTOS BY ARTIST

Stephen M. Braun
Guardian Angel for Oil | 2009
40 X 26 X 8 INCHES (101.6 X 66 X 20.3 CM)
Hand-built personal-recipe clay, brushed glaze, underglaze brushwork, overglazed, electric fired, smoking for reduction in straw, cones 07 and 04
PHOTO BY ARTIST

Heather McQueen
Gregory Milne
Fluted Sentinel Vessel | 2009
64 X 22 X 22 INCHES (162.6 X 55.9 X 55.9 CM)
Press-molded, hand-built, slab-built, and wheel-thrown white raku, brushed and sprayed glaze, electric and gas fired, controlled cooling, smoking for reduction, selective smoking for reduction, cone 018
PHOTO BY ALYCE HENSON

Shari Sikora
Knight Vessel | 2007
7½ X 6 X 4 INCHES (19.1 X 15.2 X 10.2 CM)
Hand-built and pressed Standard 239, brushed glaze, propane fired, smoked for reduction
PHOTO BY CAROL ROPER

Teruhiko (Terry) Hagiwara
My Cubism (III) | 2007
9½ X 9 INCHES (24.1 X 22.9 CM)
Wheel-thrown personal-recipe clay, painted glaze and gas fired, smoking for reduction
PHOTO BY JACK ZILKER

Mary Ann Nailos
Summer Solstice | 2009
10 X 7 X 1½ INCHES (25.4 X 17.8 X 3.8 CM)
Slab-built Balcones White, terra sigillata, brushed with ferric chloride, sawdust, and sugar, wrapped in aluminum foil, saggar fired, air cooled
PHOTO BY ARTIST

Steven Branfman
Vessel | 2007
16 X 11 INCHES (40.6 X 27.9 CM)
Thrown Laguna #25, brushed and splattered glaze, carved and pressed texture, propane fired, controlled cooling with water spray, reduction in wood shavings
PHOTO BY ARTIST

Karen Anne van Barneveld-Price
Raku Pagoda II | 2008
15 X 5½ X 5½ INCHES (38.1 X 14 X 14 CM)
Hand- and slab-built Soldate 60, brushed glaze,
stamped, gas fired, smoking for reduction, cone 06
PHOTO BY ARTIST

Mieke van Sambeeck
Ancient Language | 2008
6 X 6 X 6 INCHES (15.2 X 15.2 X 15.2 CM)
Wheel-thrown and hand-built stoneware, burnished, waxed, gas-raku fired
PHOTO BY ARTIST

Bob Green
V-Neck Vessel | 2005
14 X 9 X 7 INCHES (35.6 X 22.9 X 17.8 CM)
Thrown and altered Sheffield S14, sprayed glaze, porcelain slip, gas fired, reduced in wood chips, cone 06
PHOTO BY JOHN POLAK

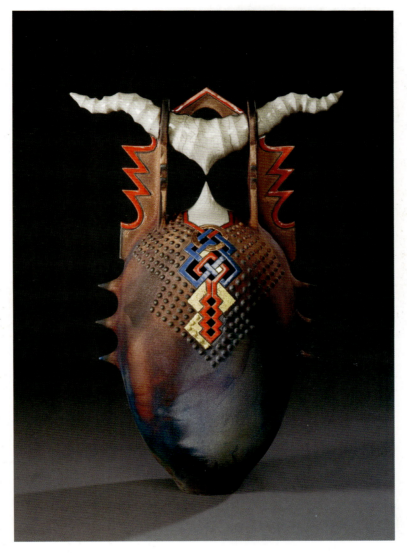

Leonid Siveriver
Horned Vessel | 2007
22 x 13 x 9 INCHES (55.9 x 33 x 22.9 CM)
Slab-built, thrown and altered raku clay with kyanite,
brushed and sprayed glaze, gold and copper leaf slip,
gas fired, controlled cooling, smoking for reduction
PHOTO BY WILLIAM VANDEVER

Deanna Pini

Black-and-White Rattles | 2007

EACH: 5 INCHES (12.7 CM) IN DIAMETER

Wheel-thrown Rod's Bod, brushed glaze, stencil, wax resist, gas fired, smoking for reduction

PHOTO BY ARTIST

David Charles Beeching
Libby | 2008
6 X 2½ X 7 INCHES (15.2 X 6.4 X 17.8 CM)
Hand-built low-fire Amaco Indian Red Clay No. 67, underglaze, hand-dusted oxides, gold luster, cone 05 glaze, raku fired, smoked/cooled in garbage canister with lit newspaper
PHOTO BY ARTIST

John Thigpen
Pod | 2007

6 X 11 X 9½ INCHES (15.2 X 27.9 X 24.1 CM)
Hand-built and pinched standard ceramic supply #182 stoneware, naked raku, glaze over slip resist, gas fired, sawdust reduction, cleaned, hand-waxed finish, cone 015
PHOTO BY ARTIST

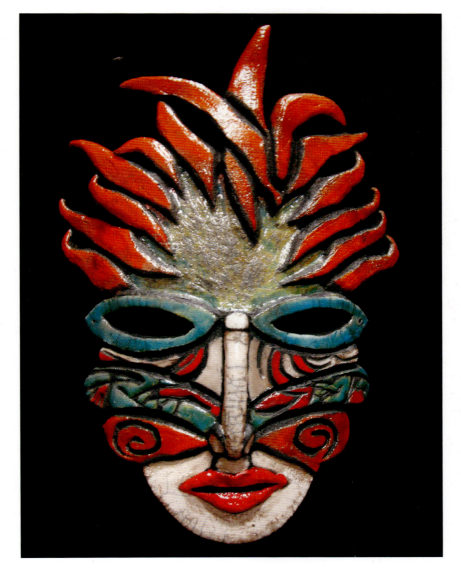

Philip Gordon Newman
Cultural Mask | 2008

13½ X 10 X ½ INCHES (34.3 X 25.4 X 1.3 CM)
Hand- and slab-built Three Finger Jack commercial clay, brushed glaze, carved, stamped, electric fired, controlled cooling, smoking for reduction

PHOTO BY ARTIST

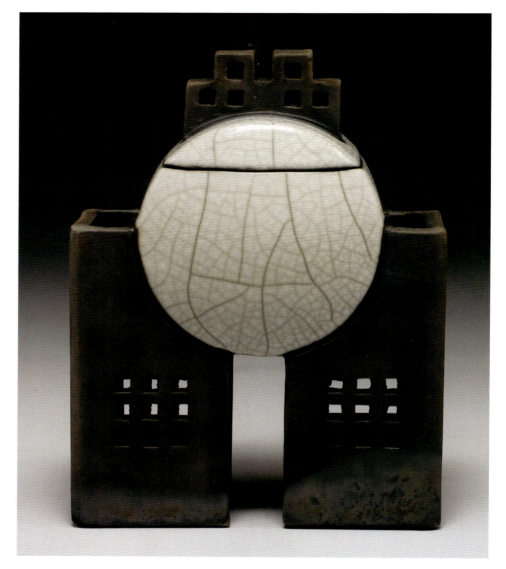

Steve Vachon
Temple Vessel | 2006
7½ X 5½ X 3¼ INCHES (19.1 X 14 X 8.3 CM)
Hand-built and slab-built personal-recipe clay, sprayed glaze, gas fired, smoking for reduction
PHOTO BY ARTIST

Barbara Harnack
Rocking Horse | 2009
75 X 19 X 10 INCHES (190.5 X 48.3 X 25.4 CM)
Relief-sculpted, hand-built, and slab-built Laguna Big White Stoneware, brushed glaze, underglaze brushwork, overglazed, incised, marking, gas fired, smoking for reduction in straw
PHOTO BY ARTIST

Hongwei Li
Self-Portrait #10 | 2006
12 X 11 X 8 INCHES (30.5 X 27.9 X 20.3 CM)
Slab-built earthenware, brushed glaze, gas fired, smoking in reduction, cone 06
PHOTO BY ARTIST

Carole Fleischman
Todd Flaky Paws | 2008
4 X 9½ X 3½ INCHES (10.2 X 24.1 X 8.9 CM)
Sculpted, extruded, hand, and slab-built white stoneware, brushed glaze, terra sigillata, carved, raku kiln fired, horsehair reduction, polished
PHOTO BY ARTIST

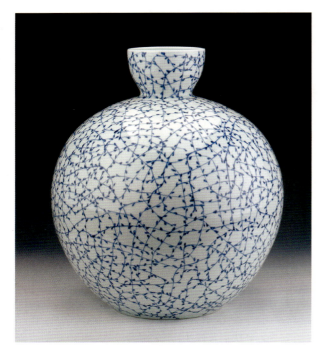

Bai Ming
Endless Life | 2008

20⁷⁄₁₆ X 17⁵⁄₁₆ INCHES (52 X 44 CM)

Thrown and altered Jingdezhen Clay, sprayed glaze, underglaze brushwork, gas fired, controlled cooling, selective smoking for reduction

PHOTO BY ARTIST

Wendy DeLeon
Raku Ball | 2005

3 X 3 X 3 INCHES (7.6 X 7.6 X 7.6 CM)

Wheel-thrown Soldate 60, brushed glaze, stamped, gas fired, smoking for reduction

PHOTO BY ARTIST

Michael Sheba
Icon Series 1 | 2007
7 x 4¼ x 3 INCHES (17.8 X 10.8 X 7.6 CM)
Hand-built and assembled PSH Sheba Raku with
fossilized stone, burnished, sgraffito, 24-karat gold leaf,
propane-fired raku, smoking for reduction, cone 06
PHOTO BY ARTIST

Stephen M. Braun
Talking Trash | 2007
43 X 30 X 7 INCHES (109.2 X 76.2 X 17.8 CM)
Hand-built personal-recipe clay, brushed glaze, underglaze brushwork, oxide wash, overglazed, electric fired, smoking for reduction in straw, cones 07 and 04
PHOTO BY ARTIST

Erin Essin Campbell
Raku Teapot | 2007
8½ x 10½ x 2½ INCHES (21.6 X 26.7 X 6.4 CM)
Hand-built and slab-built Highwater Clay, brushed glaze, stamped, electric fired raku, smoking for reduction

PHOTO BY ARTIST

Mark Yudell
Nus | 2007
6 X 4 X 6½ INCHES (15.2 X 10.2 X 16.5 CM)
Hand-built Vingerling-129, dipped glaze, underglaze brushwork, gas fired, smoking for reduction
PHOTO BY ARTIST

Patricia Murillo-Lopez
Heritage (Herencias) | 2007
15 X 11 INCHES (38.1 X 27.9 CM)
Hand-built personal-recipe clay, brushed glaze, overglaze, luster, electric fired, quick cooling in water, smoking for reduction, cone 02

PHOTO BY JAIME CISNEROS

Ruth Reese
Tom Waggle
Jim Ibur
CREATED WITH THE ASSISTANCE OF 17 APPRENTICE ARTISTS FROM ST. LOUIS ARTWORKS INC. SUMMER PROGRAM.

Missouri Foundation for Health Mural | 2009
6 X 8 FEET (1.8 X 2.4 M)
Slab-built, hand-cut, and framed stoneware, brushed glaze, underglazes, carved, stamped, underglaze brushwork, raku fired, smoking for reduction
PHOTO BY ARTISTS

Kelly Edwards
Internal Transport | 2009
30 × 13 INCHES (76.2 × 33 CM)
Hand-built raku, brushed glaze, carved,
gas fired, smoking for reduction, cone 06
PHOTO BY ARTIST

Jim Romberg
Journey's Map | 2009

About the Juror

Jim Romberg has been working with raku ceramics for more than 50 years. A professor emeritus of ceramics and a studio artist, he exhibits and gives workshops on raku throughout the United States and Europe. Romberg is a member of the International Academy of Ceramics and a board member of the National Council on Education in the Ceramic Arts (NCECA).

Over the years, Romberg has developed post-firing reduction treatments that enhance a painterly use of glaze and slips on both wheel-thrown and hand-built work. He has published articles in *Ceramics*, *Art and Perception*, *Ceramics Monthly*, and *American Craft*. His work has been featured in numerous books, including *Mastering Raku* by Steven Branfman. Romberg lives in Abiquiu, New Mexico, where the landscape, geology, and mix of cultures provide inspiration for his art.

Acknowledgments

Juror and ceramist Jim Romberg is artist in residence at the Eagleheart Center for Art and Inquiry in Abiquiu, New Mexico. He is a longtime advocate and champion for raku. I thank him for the enthusiasm, joyful spirit, and expertise he brought to the project.

I'm similarly grateful to all the ceramists who submitted images of their amazing work for the book. It was a privilege and a joy to review it all, which reflects so well the vibrancy of the raku work being done today. Thank you for your generosity in sharing your talents.

At Lark Crafts, the editorial team of Julie Hale, Dawn Dillingham, Larry Shea, and Valerie Anderson, and the art team of Matt Shay, Kristi Pfeffer, and Shannon Yokeley offered excellent and invaluable efforts. Writing for all of us, I hope you enjoy the book, and that the diverse, innovative work represented on these pages expands your idea of what raku is and what it can be.

— **Ray Hemachandra, senior editor**

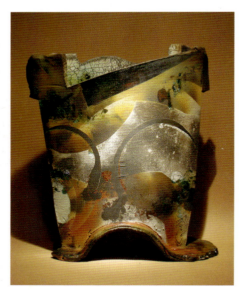

Jim Romberg
Signal Light | 2005

Contributing Artists

A

Abe, Tomoko Amaki Rye, New York, 325
Adelaar, Karen Gail Hopewell Junction, New York, 314
Aertker, Mirtha Dallas, Texas, 121
Agarwal, Vineeta D. Redmond, Washington, 270
Aiello, Rosemary New City, New York, 182
Al, Shirley Elora, Ontario, Canada, 195
Aldrich, Sally Ridgefield, Connecticut, 323
Allan, Ruth E. Wenatchee, Washington, 118
Allee, Jake R. Grand Junction, Colorado, 295
Allen, Steven San Francisco, California, 163
Alliband, Kay Carlingford, Australia, 331
Anderson, Ariella Ein Ayala, Israel, 319, 336
Anderson, Julie Kristin Steamboat Springs, Colorado, 141
Angel-Wing, Dina Berkeley, California, 237
Apkariah, Wilson H. New Braunfels, Texas, 18
Arcidiacono, JoLea S. San Marcos, Texas, 327
Armstrong, Anne Louise Waterford, Ontario, Canada, 100
Armstrong, John P. Willow Grove, Pennsylvania, 135
Ashbaugh, Sandy Chandler, Arizona, 326
Asselberghs, Wally Lille, Belgium, 209
Aulerich, Steve Corvallis, Oregon, 161
Axford, JoAnn F. Glenmont, New York, 48, 373

B

Balcazar, Miriam Van Nuys, California, 165
Bartmann, Sharon Ardmore, Pennsylvania, 139
Baskin, Shane Charlotte, North Carolina, 199
Bassett, James Northampton, England, 129
Battiato, Joseph J. San Jose, California, 80
Beall, Jane Chula Vista, California, 291
Beardall, Colette Metcalfe, Ontario, Canada, 337
Beck, Sarah Englishtown, Nova Scotia, Canada, 344
Beckett, Robin Gail Statesville, North Carolina, 44
Beeching, David Charles Fort Myers, Florida, 401
Berndt, Nicki Humble, Texas, 178
Bielenstein-Morich, Cordula Fengersfors, Sweden, 350
Booe, Lisa Marie Evansville, Indiana, 322
Bourke, Deanna Lee Chula Vista, California, 328
Boyer-Sebern, Jo-Michele Fallbrook, California, 135
Branfman, Steven Newton, Massachusetts, 28, 388, 396
Brannin, Maryke Suren Glendale, California, 169
Brauhn, Molly I. Yuma, Arizona, 312
Braun, Stephen M. Whitefish, Montana, 392, 410
Bray, Shari Las Vegas, Nevada, 30, 380
Brazelton, Jennifer San Francisco, California, 270
Bridges, Eunice Plano, Texas, 315
Bright, Matthew Eden Prairie, Minnesota, 218
Broad, Jessica Savannah, Georgia, 183
Broderick, Susan Selden, New York, 104
Broome, Tracey Chapel Hill, North Carolina, 114
Brown, Reg Springfield, Virginia, 217
Budas, Jon San Jose, California, 204
Buraud, Philippe A. Fontenay-lés-Briis, France, 25, 382
Burton, E. Tyler Los Angeles, California, 120

C

Camargo, Bia São Paulo, Brazil, 12
Camarillo II, Ramon Vienna, Virginia, 154
Campbell, Erin Essin Black Mountain, North Carolina, 411
Canupp, Phyllis Elizabeth Virginia Beach, Virginia, 231
Carcia, Joan Reading, Massachusetts, 177
Casarella, Candy Atlanta, Georgia, 98
Case, Karen A. Longboat Key, Florida, 69, 156
Chambers, Michael Jones Tiffin, Ohio, 211
Chang, Jao-O Beatrice Livingston, New Jersey, 222
Chang-Kue, Gem Gabriola Island, British Columbia, Canada, 28
Cherichetti, Avis Akers Granby, Connecticut, 201
Chianelli, John S. Prior Lake, Minnesota, 192
Choplet, Nadeige Brooklyn, New York, 258
Ciccia, Maria Antonietta Arena-Metato, Italy, 292
Clifford, Shirley Ingersoll, Ontario, Canada, 44
Clopatofsky, Irina Velasco Springfield, Michigan, 54, 375
Clyatt, Bob Rye, New York, 253
Cockrell, Rita Ruth Columbia, South Carolina, 66
Cohen, Patricia Albuquerque, New Mexico, 138
Cole, Donna Aloha, Oregon, 277
Collins, David T. Douglasville, Georgia, 216
Connell, Jim Rock Hill, South Carolina, 87, 382
Conner, Lisa Hueil Cincinnati, Ohio, 99
Corbett, Natasha Elizabeth Launceston, Australia, 332
Cosby, Leigh Prescott, Arizona, 239
Cox, Betsy Glen Dale, West Virginia, 90
Cramer, Nancy Louise North Vancouver, British Columbia, Canada, 58
Crane, David Blacksburg, Virginia, 31
Cream, Jamie Lynn Cherry Hill, New Jersey, 122
Currie, Ann Sterlington, Louisiana, 259

D

Dangora, Denise Huntington Beach, California, 146
Danhieux, Alistair Saint-Amand-en-Puisaye, France, 101
Davis, Josse Arundel, England, 53
de Beer, Liz Gibsons, British Columbia, Canada, 57
de la Cruz, Frederick San Diego, California, 262
Deal, Boni Camas, Washington, 110
Deal, Dave Camas, Washington, 110
DeLeon, Wendy Whittier, California, 408
Demme, Laura L. Wyndmoor, Pennsylvania, 191
deSaillan, Holly Sean Asheville, North Carolina, 162
Deschamps, Dorothy Louise Montreal, Quebec, Canada, 214
Diedrich, Jana Lakewood, Colorado, 68, 158
Dinnen, Gerry Carnegie, Pennsylvania, 136
Dodeja, Reena Portland, Oregon, 278
Doherty, Linda Burnaby, British Columbia, Canada, 32
Dreizin, Nurit Yokneam, Israel, 356
Dresser, Sherry Simcoe, Ontario, Canada, 335
Dube, Katherine Westlake Village, California, 320
Dudley, Dan Carrollton, Texas, 318
Dudley, Lori Lee Carrollton, Texas, 310

Duensing, Shelby Banks West Columbia, South Carolina, 233
During, Nesrin Oosterend, Netherlands, 65
Dyer, Dawn Angela Carrollton, Georgia, 210

E

Edwards, Kelly North Little Rock, Arkansas, 415
Edwards, Vickie Atlanta, Georgia, 221
Endo, Miya Dixon, New Mexico, 52, 376
England, Ana Felicity, Ohio, 219
Epstein, Linda Cabin John, Maryland, 206
Epstein, Lindsey Dighton, Massachusetts, 246
Esquierdo, Skip San Lorenzo, California, 285
Estes, Paul Carl Kewanee, Illinois, 67
Evans, John Worthing, England, 257
Even-Chen, Simcha Rehovot, Israel, 74, 269

F

Faktorowich, Sharon Ramat Ef'al, Israel, 363
Farmer, Lynda Albany, Oregon, 207
Feige, James Robert San Mateo, California, 273
Feld, Julia Nicole San Jose, California, 19
Ferrell, Emily E. Borger, Texas, 276
Fetterman, Beverly Helaine Dallas, Texas, 224
Finocchi, Ilena Stockton, California, 81
Fisher, Frank James Milford, Michigan, 274, 362
Fleischman, Carole Irving, Texas, 64, 407
Flock, Christopher Reid Hamilton, Ontario, Canada, 358
Florell, Katrina Mae Elm Creek, Nebraska, 329
Foo, Anthony J. Placentia, California, 254
Forester, Lillian Lakefield, Ontario, Canada, 343
Frazey-Jordan, Merla Coulterville, California, 112
Frazier, Birgitta Volcano, Hawaii, 366
Fritz, Don Santa Cruz, California, 94

G

Gaddy, Janet Marie Danville, Virginia, 160
Gaede, Drew Fort Collins, Colorado, 14
Gahrmann, Colleen Sweeney Spotswood, New Jersey, 327
Galligan, Mary Devon, Pennsylvania, 167
Gallo, Alessandro Genova, Italy, 8
Ganstrom, Sheldon Hays, Kansas, 132, 391
Garcia, Leticia Santa Cruz, Bolivia, 340
Gariepy, Jon Petaluma, California, 45, 125

Garrity, Wanda Port Orchard, Washington, 111
Gartner, Jo-Ann West Babylon, New York, 76
Geerts, Judy Spring Lake, Michigan, 109, 386
Getzan, Jill Helen Sunnyvale, California, 124
Gilad, Ruth Tel Aviv, Israel, 334
Gilbert, Diane Columbia, South Carolina, 240
Giles, Kristen Addison, Texas, 247
Glisson, Theresa A. Goldsboro, North Carolina, 226
Glynn, Sinéad Marie Kildare, Ireland, 47
Gould, Ronnie Bedford, Massachusetts, 180
Gray, Douglas E. Florence, South Carolina, 265
Greedy, Rosemarie Kelowna, British Columbia, Canada, 21
Green, Bob Conway, Massachusetts, 372, 398
Green, Leslie Philomath, Oregon, 11
Greener, Stef Tucson, Arizona, 309
Gushee, Rhonda Greenville, South Carolina, 390

H

Hagiwara, Teruhiko (Terry) Houston, Texas, 151, 395
Haile, Charles San Antonio, Texas, 143
Hall, Don Turlock, California, 61
Hall, Shaun Halstead, England, 168
Halls, Susan Easthampton, Massachusetts, 300
Hannigan, Teri Topanga, California, 55, 378
Harnack, Barbara Cerrillos, New Mexico, 92, 405
Harp, Paul R. Fairport, New York, 298
Harris, Cathy M. Aurora, Ontario, Canada, 352
Harris, Jackie F. Columbus, North Carolina, 38
Harris, Linda Bobcaygeon, Ontario, Canada, 116
Harvey, Wesley Eugene San Antonio, Texas, 282
Harwood, Jerel M. Orem, Utah, 299
Hawkins, Dan Bulverde, Texas, 137
Hayden, Maria Palm Beach Gardens, Florida, 147
Hayter, Joyce Pompton Plains, New Jersey, 242
Hemingway, Steven Edward Minnetonka, Minnesota, 249
Henderson, Judy Little Rock, Arkansas, 84
Hess, Richard T. Austin, Texas, 117
Hesser, Lynnette Wellington, Alabama, 234
Hilliard, Julie C. Scaly Mountain, North Carolina, 91, 360

Hole, Nina Skaelskor, Denmark, 346
Holley, Lin M. Seattle, Washington, 236
Hong, Gerald Petaluma, California, 288, 371
Hong, Kelly Petaluma, California, 288, 371
Horowitz, Carla Montclair, New Jersey, 60
Horton, Wayne Bastrop, Louisiana, 259
Hoskisson, Cindy Dallas, Oregon, 243
Hould, Zac La Verne, California, 261
Howard, Thelma Marie Saskatoon, Saskatchewan, Canada, 338
Hudin, Cathryn R. Oroville, California, 96

I

Ibur, Jim St. Louis, Missouri, 414
Ignarri, John Cherry Hill, New Jersey, 211

J

Jackson, Richard N. Reno, Nevada, 255
Jacobson, Kate Kailua-Kona, Hawaii, 289, 370
Jacobson, Will Kailua-Kona, Hawaii, 289, 370
Janssen, Marijke Amsterdam, Netherlands, 311
Jensen, Brian L. Springville, Utah, 294
Johnson, Helen Atlanta, Georgia, 205
Johnston, Deborah Toronto, Ontario, Canada, 83, 381
Johnstone, Emma Kingston upon Thames, England, 75, 333
Johnstone, Jim Portland, Oregon, 164
Jones, David Leamington Spa, England, 348

K

Kamhi, Beth R. Chicago, Illinois, 82
Karabey, Burcu Öztürk Ankara, Turkey, 13
Kasparian, Marianne Phoenix, Arizona, 39
Kawalez, Marlene Angela Milton, Ontario, Canada, 159
Kellogg, Nina Studio City, California, 193
Kellum, John J. Orlando, Florida, 229
Kirchmer, Susan Escondido, California, 67
Kryger, Elaine Klaasen Plano, Texas, 78
KW, Diane Honolulu, Hawaii, 266

L

Lancaster, Michael Cerrillos, New Mexico, 93, 384
Lauriat, Alison Concord, Massachusetts, 108
Laws, Leslie Ann McKinney, Texas, 43
Lawson, Richard Kenmore, Washington, 272
Lea, Jeremy Barton Danville, Virginia, 181
Lee, Teri Oakland, California, 194
Lees, Emily Jo Chapel Hill, North Carolina, 25, 383

Leibman, Amourentia Louisa North Vancouver, British Columbia, Canada, 339
Lepkin, Irit Toronto, Ontario, Canada, 151
Lesins, Dainis Riga, Latvia, 340
Leuthold, Marc Potsdam, New York, 79
Lewis, Leslie Laine Lubbock, Texas, 197
Li, Hongwei Beijing, China, 63, 406
Ligtenberg, Swanica Los Altos Hills, California, 146
Lin, Jack Yingge, Taiwan, 358
Lindberg, Mia Jensen Beach, Florida, 220
Lindquist, Renee Elizabeth League City, Texas, 153
Lintner, Falina Sinopah Whitefish, Montana, 306
Linton, Andrew Patrick Charlotte, North Carolina, 198
Litvany, Monica Pompton Lakes, New Jersey, 385
Lockett, Chérie Robin Evanston, Illinois, 281
Loucks, Steve Wellington, Alabama, 231
Lurie, Gale Seattle, Washington, 355
Lusardi, Mark New Richmond, Wisconsin, 367

M

Magaldi, Jessica Brooklyn, New York, 157
Mahaffey, Tom St. Charles, Illinois, 309
Mahoney, Karen Needham, Massachusetts, 351
Malebranche, Genez Gilley Virginia Beach, Virginia, 218
Malson, Donna Hunt, Texas, 283
Malson, Ken Hunt, Texas, 267
Manfredi, Justin R. Reno, Nevada, 208
Mangham, Billy Ray San Marcos, Texas, 248
Manna, Jim Geneva, Illinois, 232
Marbach, Linda Louise East Quogue, New York, 279
Maron, Loren Ossining, New York, 157
Mars, Gina Huntington Station, New York, 36, 377
Marsh, Ginny Rockwall, Texas, 293
Marshall, Lambeth Walker Waxhaw, North Carolina, 51, 375
Matsui, Keiko Bondi Junction, Australia, 341
Mau, Linda Hansen Saratoga, California, 73, 256
McCall, Gale Inglewood, California, 353
McCartney, Margot Laguna Woods, California, 22
McDaniel, Eileen Wautoma, Wisconsin, 177
McDonald, Jane Petaluma, California, 80

McGourlick, Sylvia Shiu-Wai Campbell River, British Columbia, Canada, 130
McQueen, Heather Chicago, Illinois, 145, 393
Merida-Paytes, Lisa Cincinnati, Ohio, 97, 387
Miller, Hasuyo V. Temecula, California, 37
Miller, Judy Bolef Lafayette, California, 317
Miller, K. Sam The Colony, Texas, 287
Milne, Gregory Chicago, Illinois, 145, 393
Minc, Iris Merrimac, Massachusetts, 57
Ming, Bai Beijing, China, 408
Miranti, Bob New Rochelle, New York, 107, 321
Missett, Kate Brooklyn, New York, 324
Mitchell, John Patrick Central Falls, Rhode Island, 189
Moore, Ritsuko Summit, New Jersey, 86
Moran, Timothy Winspear Danville, Virginia, 173
Moren, Richard Anthony Del Mar, California, 303
Moriah-Winik, Alma Nehora, Israel, 35
Morris, Paul F. Fort Collins, Colorado, 239
Moss, Rhea Lake Worth, Florida, 105
Mull, Tom San Francisco, California, 41
Murillo-Lopez, Patricia La Paz, Bolivia, 413
Murray, Alyson L. Newmarket, Ontario, Canada, 34
Myers, Kevin Arthur Santa Ana, California, 313

N

Nailos, Mary Ann Cedar Park, Texas, 140, 395
Nauman, Eric John St. Louis, Missouri, 305
Neish, Frances Toronto, Ontario, Canada, 110
Newman, Philip Gordon Bend, Oregon, 403
Nimmo, Audrey Stoney Creek, Ontario, Canada, 77
Ninh, Cac Los Angeles, California, 314
Nuti, Chiara Cecina, Italy, 140

O

O'Donnell, Laura Urbana, Illinois, 307
Obodzinski, Mary Carolyn Crystal Lake, Illinois, 134
Onodera, Aki Barcelona, Spain, 17
Orwin, Gerri Toronto, Ontario, Canada, 354

P

Pacin, Phyllis Oakland, California, 174
Pappas, Evamarie Nashville, Tennessee, 263
Parent, Janine Quebec City, Quebec, Canada, 33, 378

Parisi, Gino Potomac, Maryland, 118
Park, Joel Honolulu, Hawaii, 266
Parr, David P. Brighton, Michigan, 295
Pasenow, Liz Hamilton, Ontario, Canada, 62, 379
Paulet, Vicki Rapport Dunwoody, Georgia, 71, 212
Pené, Nancy Upland, California, 23
Peters, Laura Albany, Oregon, 128
Pevarnik, Joan Vail, Arizona, 185
Pfanstiehl, Nina Hope Newport, Rhode Island, 347
Phelps, Kathy Atlanta, Georgia, 102
Pilo, Shuli Closter, New Jersey, 283
Pini, Deanna Santa Barbara, California, 400
Popova, Biliana La Crescenta, California, 359
Powell, Joan A. Pacific, Missouri, 87
Price, Julia Larkin Louisville, Colorado, 170
Priestley, Jo Mission, British Columbia, Canada, 357
Prince, Cynthia L. Duluth, Georgia, 106
Proctor-Givens, Marilyn Tallahassee, Florida, 230
Prokos, Michael Placitas, New Mexico, 15
Putsch-Grassi, Karin Reggello, Italy, 364

R

Rasmussen, Elaine Castro Valley, California, 345
Ratcliff, Gary L. Monroe, Louisiana, 244
Razmakhova, Inna San Jose, California, 277
Redding, Yasmine Las Vegas, Nevada, 302
Reese, Ruth Kirkwood, Missouri, 414
Reese, Ruth Ann St. Louis, Missouri, 223
Rehbein, Catherine J. Monroe, Michigan, 205
Reinking III, John A. Hellertown, Pennsylvania, 201
Reiver, Marcia Rosemont, Pennsylvania, 185
Resende, Yola Vale Proença-A-Nova, Portugal, 72, 345
Richardson, Julee Oakland, California, 142
Rieger, Martha Tel Aviv, Israel, 24
Rodgers, Deborah G. Ft. Worth, Texas, 171
Roest-Chapman, Truus Montreal, Quebec, Canada, 42
Roitich, Gennady Hod HaSharon, Israel, 94
Rossman, Carol Dundas, Ontario, Canada, 71, 203
Ruggiero, Nici Hertfordshire, England, 46
Rukavina, Jadranka Zagreb, Croatia, 365
Rushmore, Gail Redwood Valley, California, 225

Russell, Carol Prescott, Arizona, 144
Ryan, Erin El Cajon, California, 179

S

Sachs, Barb Dundas, Ontario, Canada, 166, 369
Sampson, Debra Katz Deerfield, Illinois, 264
Sanchez, Steven Aloha, Oregon, 252
Sausa, Ilona Daugavpils, Latvia, 190
Savignac, Dora A. Severna Park, Maryland, 187
Scanlan, Cathleen Warren, Rhode Island, 175
Schembri, David Newmarket, Ontario, Canada, 251
Schillaci, Joellen Varsalona Stuart, Florida, 235
Schneider, Helaine Orlando, Florida, 27
Schran, William R. Fredericksburg, Virginia, 100
Schwarz, Jeffrey A. Pittsburgh, Pennsylvania, 194
Scott, Sam Shoreline, Washington, 95, 316
Sell, Dale Chula Vista, California, 242
Selsor, Marcia L. Brownsville, Texas, 250
Shackleton, Cher Mosman Park, Australia, 123
Shafran, Daryl Los Altos, California, 202
Shaver, Bonnie Rae South Salem, New York, 133
Sheba, Michael Toronto, Ontario, Canada, 361, 409
Shelley, Suzanne Sydney, Australia, 126
Shiber, Mona Michelle Northampton, Massachusetts, 184
Showalter, Jesse Lake Worth, Florida, 85
Sikora, Shari Drexel Hill, Pennsylvania, 260, 394
Silberlicht, Ellen Honesdale, Pennsylvania, 56
Sillem, Pia Vancouver, British Columbia, Canada, 103
Siveriver, Leonid Roosevelt, New Jersey, 29, 399
Skog, Lisa Joanne Grimsby, Ontario, Canada, 20
Smeraldo, Carol East Preston, Nova Scotia, Canada, 268
Smith, David Scott Kalispell, Montana, 188
Smith, DeWitt Watkinsville, Georgia, 49
Spytkowska, Jola Forest Gate, England, 286
St. Clair, Krysia Bermagui, Australia, 115
Stankus, Martin Raleigh, North Carolina, 227
Stearns, Eric L. Crete, Nebraska, 150

Stellaccio, Anthony E. Crownsville, Maryland, 50, 374
Stockdale, Scott Kristian Manteo, North Carolina, 215
Stonis, Dinah Sheeran Atlanta, Georgia, 200
Strauss, Stevens Oakland, California, 148
Stumpf, Suzanne South Natick, Massachusetts, 224
Summer, Roland Velden, Austria, 290
Sutter, Lorraine Saskatoon, Saskatchewan, Canada, 290
Sweet, Marvin Merrimac, Massachusetts, 70, 176

T

Takahashi, Reid Glendale, California, 263
Tambe, Priya Rye, New York, 127
Tanzer, Joan Piedmont, California, 196
Taylor, Kara West Palm Beach, Florida, 213
Tebbens, Marianne G. Radnor, Pennsylvania, 89
Testa, Ann Orinda, California, 119
Testa, Teresa Las Vegas, Nevada, 308
Thigpen, John Decatur, Georgia, 402
Thomas, Ian F. Butler, Pennsylvania, 284
Timco, Lance Andrew Colorado Springs, Colorado, 302
Tomczyk-Jackson, Tammy South Portland, Maine, 241
Tomkins, George Yuma, Arizona, 96, 388
Trauttmansdorff, Gise Jerseyville, Ontario, Canada, 349
Trotter, Glenn Prescott, Arizona, 238
Truitt, Penny Santa Fe, New Mexico, 26, 389

V

Vachon, Steve Fort Wayne, Indiana, 10, 404
Vaisgur, Sigal Shoham, Israel, 296
Valentine, Jack W. Hartville, Ohio, 228
van Barneveld-Price, Karen Anne Prescott, Arizona, 40, 397
van Sambeeck, Mieke Maleny, Australia, 398
Van Veen, Ri Williamstown, Victoria, Australia, 334
Vastila, Rose Kadera Two Harbors, Minnesota, 59
Venhuizen, Von Lubbock, Texas, 149
Viala, Michel Louis Pigeon Hill, Quebec, Canada, 164
Villaverde, Vilma Buenos Aires, Argentina, 347
Vivas, Chris Ronkonkoma, New York, 304

W

Waggle, Tom St. Louis, Missouri, 414
Wallace, Kenneth Michael Mountain View, California, 131
Ward, Nina de Creeft Santa Barbara, California, 152
Webb, Nathan C. Bethel, Vermont, 113
Weir, Catherine Hamilton, Ontario, Canada, 355
Weiss, Mark S. Nyack, New York, 171
Westby, Lars Baltimore, Maryland, 155
Wharton, Candone Marie Daytona Beach Shores, Florida, 88
Whitehand, Dawn Dunnstown, Victoria, Australia, 330
Whitfill, Patrick M. Spartanburg, South Carolina, 284
Willard, Linda St. Albert, Alberta, Canada, 172
Williams, Cynthia J. Tulsa, Oklahoma, 245
Wilson, Betty L. West Palm Beach, Florida, 186
Winters, Travis Buffalo, New York, 275
Wirun, Peter Toronto, Ontario, Canada, 368
Wood, Pamela Ridgewood, New Jersey, 271
Woodrow, Julie Marysville, Ohio, 9
Worley, Susan Clare Mountain View, California, 280
Wortman, Susan Sleepy Hollow, New York, 128
Wysong, Pete Boulder, Colorado, 297

Y

Yamaguchi, Susan San Mateo, California, 321
Yamauchi, Mori Kentish Town, England, 342
Yardley, Valerie King of Prussia, Pennsylvania, 58
Yarnold, Mike Decatur, Georgia, 16
Yoganathan, Tripti Tucker, Georgia, 124
Yokel, Fred Campbell, California, 301
Yudell, Mark Pardes Hanna-Karkur, Israel, 412

Z

Zarbock, Nancy Pittstown, New Jersey, 50
Zavala, Juan Manuel Spring Valley, California, 255